The Silver Linings

Storybook
VOLUME 2

10 Health & Happiness Professionals Share Inspiring Stories of Overcoming Stormy Days in Personal & Professional Life

DEBBIE HOROVITCH

Copyright © 2016 Social Sparkle & Shine

All Rights Reserved

Published by Debbie Horovitch of Social Sparkle & Shine

No part of this publication may be reproduced, or stored in a retrieval system, or transmitted in any form or by any means, electronic, mechanical, recording, photocopying, scanning or otherwise, without express written permission of the publisher.

For information about permission to reproduce selections from this book, email the publisher Debbie Horovitch at debbie.horovitch@gmail.com or visit our website at www.theSparkleAgency.com

PUBLISHER'S DISCLAIMER
While the publisher and coauthors have used their best efforts in preparing this book, they make no representations or warranties with respect to the accuracy or completeness of the contents of this book. No warranty may be created or extended by sales representatives or written sales materials. The advice and strategies contained herein may not be suitable for your situation. You should consult with a professional where appropriate. Neither the publisher nor author shall be liable for any loss of profit or any other commercial damages, including but not limited to special, incidental, consequential, or other damages.

Cover design concept Nathan Johnson
Cover design Sandra Jean-Pierre

Library and Archive Canada Cataloging-in-Publications Data:

ISBN-13: 978-1-77316-003-0
ISBN-10: 978-1-77316-002-3 (ebk.)

Created and produced in Toronto, Ontario, Canada

FIRST EDITION

Acknowledgements

All published books have the same intent and purpose - to enlighten our readers and create a new way of looking at our life. In The Silver Linings Storybook, we look specifically at the experiences we all have in life, that highlight the positive benefits gained only from going through an evolution as we resolve and overcome our struggles, challenges, disappointments and humiliations.

The bottom line is always that while personal transformation can come easily, it more often comes following a sudden and complete change of thinking. There will be a catalyst, a trigger for change, sent in advance of each breakthrough idea or advancement.

This book is a demonstration of the potential each of us has for complete transformation. The shift in thinking, eating, and engagement that takes place, to empower our larger life dreams of significance and legacy.

To the people who had a dream but lost their sparkle along the way. This book is the result of me not listening to all the people who told me I shouldn't, or couldn't, or would regret my choices, as I explore my potential in life—I hope you'll follow my example and explore your own passion project to bring forward into the world. Thank you to everyone who has supported my curious and testing approach over the years, and stayed nearby even through my disasters, to enjoy the benefits of a storytelling approach to producing small business info-products as a form of media inventory.

Thank you to all the successful book authors and business leaders who have so generously shared their most valuable insights & advice, and success stories with their communities of readers, and myself as they grow. Dorie Clark, Mike Michalowicz, Michael Procopio, Michael Chartrand, and Keith McDevitt: without your friendship, advice, and encouragement over the years, I could not be here now. Jack Mize, Brian Horne, and all my colleagues in book publishing & media. Thank you for leading the way with bright ideas and encouragement through the stormy times.

Thank you to all the people and who have gone out of their way to remind me that I am not invisible, powerless, or insignificant even during the times when it seems like I must be.

Debbie Horovitch

Silver Linings Storybook Coauthors

Volume 2

Fall 2016

Angela Sidlo

Chris Holley

Debbie Horovitch

Henry Balzani

Kathy Jalali

Kathy Kastner

Lisa Laura

Persia Cuellar

Tracey Battle

A Note From Debbie Horovitch

Your Publisher and "Fairy Godmother"

What holds us back from living up to our dreams? For most of us, it's some form of a feeling of unworthiness that holds us back from living up to our full potential, and living a life that could leave a legacy for all of humanity.

Dr. John Dimartini, the world renowned speaker, transformational leader and polymath (you likely remember him from the book and movie, The Secret) says that it's our held-onto guilt and shame that causes us to live an inauthentic life; our ego covers our shame over being imperfect and not living up to the expectations of ourselves, or of others. When we're hiding, denying the truth daily about who we are, where we come from, what we've experienced, what we've learned from it, and what is important to us moving forward—these are the root causes of all that self-destructive and addictive behaviors that we can get caught up in.

To resolve this instantly and let go, he says to write out an exhaustive list (he suggests 200!) of all the times in our lives when something happened where we harbor feelings of anger over being wronged by someone, or that we feel guilt over, or shameful of that experience, and next to each of those events to document how we were actually BEING OF SERVICE to someone or ourselves in those situations, or in the aftermath. The act of doing this can help document a new positive emotion tied to that memory, offering healing of the lasting guilt and shame, letting go of the burdens that hold us back from living authentically, and unapologetically exploring our destinies. And once we're rid of the limiting beliefs within the old story (the rules), we can tell our story again and again to generate true and lasting wealth, from embracing our story as valuable, simply because it is uniquely our own.

I have found this to be true and found myself naturally connecting with people through the practice of storytelling in my own life. I've always taken a Pollyanna view and recently started focusing on silver linings stories, after coming out of a 2-year recurrence of depression, that followed the sudden passing of a close family member.

A common theme I found in my coauthors' stories and realized exists also within myself, is that to some level, we're all conditioned to wait for permission, before beginning to live every day making more of an impact with our lives, authentically being in our passion and purpose, constantly increasing our significance to ourselves and others.

Most of us follow this rule out of habit because work, school, community, and especially families, all have unspoken rules of engagement, often about etiquette, respect, or privacy (oh, those skeletons in the closet!).

Especially in Canada, where our culture is to be so overly polite that Olympic Gold winning athlete Mark McKoy would say that we have absolutely no culture for winning. His own silver linings story is that in the minutes after he won gold in hurdles in the Barcelona Summer Olympics in 1992, after so many Olympic attempts that he was introduced as the "perennial also-ran" due to his multiple 4th place finishes at global competitions, the Canadian television Olympic commentators were so stunned that they were silent for 17 seconds of live television air time, absent of the words to express their delight at his win, at which time the best word they could muster was "unbelievable!"

While our coauthors are from around the world, each leading their own revolution of personal awareness where they are, I'm fighting against that cultural limiting belief that we need to be liked by everyone, to follow "the rules of success" that don't really exist, except in our own minds—from the global HQ of Canada.

The Silver Linings Storybook is an anthology book compiled with personal stories of the authors' own silver linings story, with the intention of empowering and inspiring the people around them who read this book, to become more generous, compassionate, and resilient in their own lives—Simply by reading and sharing Silver Linings Storybook, and talking about other silver linings stories. By holding space for faith that what we cannot see physically right now, but that can be experienced fully in our imagination, can and WILL become true with persistent action—and this applies to all of us: readers, coauthors, colleagues, and even myself as the publisher.

This book is great for passing the time during your daily commute, to include in holiday roundup reading lists, or as a gift for anyone who could use a little extra magic in their life.

The name Silver Linings Storybook comes from the proverb of "Every cloud has a silver lining", and the idea that breakthrough ideas and transformation happen for all of us, usually following a period of dramatically disrupted personal values.

Throughout our history we can see how common it is that a massive life breakthrough comes on the heels of a significant struggle or loss. The world's greatest achieved athletes, artists, and entrepreneurs/inventors all struggled with disability of confidence and support, or lack of responsibility for internal and external resources (most were told they'd never amount to anything in life, and certainly not realize any level of significance)—and many would agree that it was that experience of struggle that forced them to become a greater person, to live up to any and all surprise challenges they faced—whether they won or lost initially, it was all viewed a necessary practice to qualify, and win.

Ultimately with every attempt they were growing stronger and giving permission to everyone around them to do the same.

These stories are shared as proof that the magic, and the miracles, are happening all around each of us every day, and if we just honestly look for them, we'll begin to see them everywhere in increasing certainty, frequency, and relevance.

What is your silver linings story? Do you have more than one? Most people start off thinking that it's a story of visible success already recognized by the outside world, and that without that obvious societal "win", that they have no silver linings story worthy of telling. But I would say they are wrong! I believe that every person has a silver linings story, in fact, many (both in your past and in your future) and if you just take the time to honestly consider, without ego or prejudice, where you are holding onto an experience of trauma, prolonged struggle, humiliation, or loss... And when you look at it more closely to see where that experience actually served you and prepared you to be of more impact, now and in your future, that is when you begin to take responsibility, and earn credit, and own the value of the experience, in a way that only you can...

Whenever you share your silver linings stories, in any way, and any format, we all win. In the following chapters you'll find personal stories, many of which are being shared publicly for the very first time. Without intending it, almost all the coauthors of this volume of Silver Linings Storybook are health, business, career and success coaches—so they can help guide you through almost any life challenge you're facing.

Organically, their stories came together to touch on three common areas in life where many of us harbor a deep desire to achieve, but still struggle:
- Self-Acceptance
- Physical Transformation
- Spiritual Growth

The very first story you will read is of special significance to me and I hope to you as well. After reading her story, I encourage you to take a few minutes to reach out to her, and to the authors whose chapters you connect with, with your own silver linings story.

If you know someone who is struggling with a similar situation to any of our author stories (at a time when it might be almost impossible for them to realize the silver lining to their story), or if you would like to make a gift of books to any specific organization that continuously helps people triumph over their demons in life, please reach out to me or to your local contributor or coauthor.

While this book is not intended to replace any professional medical, legal, or tax advice in our reader's life, our Silver Linings Storybook coauthors are all available to share their own stories in person with clear relevance to your audiences at conferences and fundraising events, as well as organizational leadership and management trainings; and for fun and compelling storytelling interviews with media channels.

Learning to see your silver linings stories and express them in writing and speaking can often be an experience that is both liberating and emotionally challenging—offering you a rich well of creativity and innovation, and a steep learning curve into your own capability and potential (through the challenges), that is available to you anytime you want to begin, or continue to explore it.

If you'd like to increase your own personal impact and significance, or for your organization, by supporting Silver Linings Storybook with your story, or if you'd like copies of the book for an upcoming event, please get in touch with me or any of our coauthors on Facebook or LinkedIn.

Debbie Horovitch
Creator & Publisher Silver Linings Storybook
Toronto, Ontario, Canada
debbie.horovitch@gmail.com
416-553-2157

Table of Contents

Acknowledgements iii

Silver Linings Storybook Coauthors v

A Note From Debbie Horovitch vii

The Stage of My Opera 1

The Stage of My Opera By Persia Cuellar 3

    About Persia Cuellar 14

Self-Acceptance 17

The Wandering Years By Kathy Jalali 19

    About Kathy Jalali 26

Where Does Wellness Begin? By Angela Sidlo 29

    About Angela Sidlo 39

Awakening Through Fear by Lisa Laura 41

    About Lisa Laura 50

If The Dream Is Big Enough, The Facts Don't Count by Henry Balzani 53

    About Henry Balzani 65

Physical Transformation 67

Acknowledging the Past, Creating the Future by Chris Holley 69

    About Chris Holley 77

Finding Your Voice Among the Voices by Tracey Battle 79

    About Tracey Battle 85

Spiritual Growth..87

A Journey From Tampons to Tombstones by Kathy Kastner............ 89

    About Kathy Kastner 94

Guidance From My Guardian Angel by Debbie Horovitch 97

    About Debbie Horovitch..109

Author Recommended Resources 111

Would You... Like to Coauthor a Book With Us? 117

What's Your Silver Linings Story? 118

The Stage of My Opera

The Stage of My Opera
By Persia Cuellar

Looking back on life, it sometimes seems like you are looking at old photographs of another person or watching a movie that you remember in some faint memory. I think of my life as a movie. Let us begin the film.

The secret service agents escorted me to the rear of the stage where the production crew then positioned me center just behind the curtain. Within a few minutes, I'd be performing for the 42nd President of the United States of America, Bill Clinton. Anxiously, I prayed to God that everything would go as well as planned, and that I would not forget the words to the song that I was about to sing. The music began to play, and the curtain began to rise, and I opened my eyes to an almost out of body experience. I could see myself on stage, breathing softly and in tune with the music, as my voice began to fly freely, singing the beautiful song, *"Nella Fantasia"* [In My Fantasy] by the great Italian composer *Ennio Morricone*'s soundtrack for the film, *"The Mission"*.

"In my fantasy I see a just world
Where everyone lives in peace and honesty
I dream of a place to live that is always free
Like a cloud that floats
Full of humanity in the depths of the soul..."

    I got lost in the moment, and saw my entire life flash in my mind. How had this little Iranian girl come from so far to sing now for the President of the United States of America amidst thousands of people? It was truly an emotional, tender, and joyous moment in my life.

    On cold winter mornings, the three-year-old had a habit of kicking off her cover, only to shiver from the cold shortly thereafter. She would then stand up and run into her parent's room, climb up on their bed and dive like a fish in between Mommy and Daddy where she belonged. She'd put her ice cold feet between mother's thighs, where her small feet would then be kissed with warmth just like the rays of the summer sun rushing through her body. She'd get lost into her comfort and fall fast asleep.

    She already knew what she wanted to be. To perform on stage, was her dream.

    At home, she enjoyed performing as if she was a famous singer. She'd play her brother's 45 RPM record player, sing along and dance to the sounds of the Beatles, Elvis Presley and many other artists. Her gift from God was a beautiful voice.

    Most importantly this little princess enjoyed playing with her best friend, Marussa, the only doll she ever had. Her older siblings would go to school and when they returned home, they'd play with the little girl, day in and day out, because nobody could get enough of her. One day, as she was walking in the neighborhood with Marussa, a neighbor's kid cruising around on his bicycle suddenly lost his balance and crashed into both of them. Sadly, Marussa received the severest of injuries, her head had broken. The little Princess cried endlessly for days but not for her own injuries, but for the broken head of her best friend. This would be the very first tragedy that marked the heart of the little girl with the greatest of sadness.

    I am that little girl, born in the summer of 1957, in the city of Uromieh located in the Northwest of Iran. My brother and sister were eleven and eight years older than me. I was the baby sister until the age of thirteen when my parents had their last child, my beautiful younger brother. My mother was a housewife. She was always busy cleaning, washing, and cooking for the family. My father was a truck driver, who was absent from home most of the time. Sometimes it would be months before we would see him again. When he was home however, he would take me everywhere with him: to the movies, and to visit friends and relatives. He'd let me hold the steering wheel of his big truck and I would pretend to be the driver. He'd buy me everything and anything I wanted. My life was happiest having my entire family around, and me being the spoiled brat.

As a child, I can remember, around the age of four perhaps, when I would become sick, my mother would take me by the hand to the local pharmacy, and with the absence of a doctor's prescription, she'd casually ask the pharmacist for a couple of Penicillin for me. Then mother would take me to a local doctor's office asking the assistant to give me an injection because I was sick and coughing all night long and I wouldn't let anybody sleep. This became and was the routine for many years. When I would get sick, I would get swollen lymph node infections with nonstop painful coughing, and for the mention, I was thinner and smaller than my age group for normal children. I was fatigued, fragile and had developed intestinal bowel syndrome (IBS) at an early age. All this contributed to me being pushed around or teased most of the time. I was popular alright; everybody made fun of me that even with the slightest breeze I'd get sick. "You're sick again", they'd tease me with laughter. I don't think my health issues were ever really taken seriously. I guess that's how it was then. Kids would fall, cry, get up again and forget all about what just happened, and that's how we were raised.

My birth name is "Yerjanik", which is an Armenian name meaning, "happy". As I grew up, however, my life was anything but happy. Most of us don't realize as our lives begin to change, how we find ourselves trapped in a hole struggling to save ourselves. In my case, my hole started at the age of eleven. My brother was accepted to a university in Tehran, the capital of Iran, where he moved from home, a good sixteen-hour drive away. The same year my sister got married, and she, too, moved to Tehran. These events left me troubled, and in search of finding myself while living with a stranger, my very own mother. Having no bond between us, I no longer had the family support and the joy that I used to have with family, and I began to hate my life!

We were raised Christian Gregorian Orthodox, which existed as a minority group in Iran at a time when the country enjoyed a lifestyle westernized with the world's latest of music and fashion. Iranians at that time lived large. They sought overseas education for their children, entertained themselves with shopping sprees in Paris, Italy, New York and traveled around the world. Iran was one of the most advanced countries of the Middle East, as well as, a leader in OPEC. This was during the time of the Shah when all religious believers, Christians, Jews, Kurdish, Sunni, Bahai, Zoroastrian could all walk respectfully and harmoniously amongst one another within the majority group, Shea Muslims.

Despite life being great in Iran at that time, there were some stern cultural beliefs that I disagreed with and quickly opposed simply because my rights were less, as a female than those of my male counterparts. I was born with the gift to sing but my family opposed supporting my talent, for it was simply not considered appropriate or decent for a girl. It was in fact, quite to the contrary; this talent was looked upon as being shameful. It was decided for me, that I would not be allowed to pursue my dreams, and I got that message loud and clear, that I would not ever talk about it again. I simply did not fit within my current society. My dreams were great but my opportunities were very limited, nevertheless, my singing always brought me the greatest joy and happiness. I had a western mentality within an Eastern world. I felt trapped, and in the wrong place for my life to go on. To escape my imprisonment and despair, I would listen to the only American radio station available and learn the latest American top 40 songs. Without knowing English to my surprise, I had learned most of the songs with quite accurate pronunciation! I would dream to be Stevie Wonder's cousin and I'd sing with Lady Barbara Streisand's "Songbird". I would sing in English, and I would sing in Italian, and I could sing songs in French and Spanish without any understanding of the languages.

As I was growing up, my chronic diseases were also growing with me. I became a 17-year-old with suicidal thoughts. I fell prey to some stress related issues such as depression, IBS (intestinal Bowel Syndrome), ulcers, asthma and then these symptoms were compounded with neck and knee injuries from a car accident that I once had. My life seemed pointless. I kept on thinking if my life and talent were truly gifts, then why weren't they being recognized and celebrated? I dropped out of high school.

The year 1977 was a big turnaround in Iran. The country was changing then, due to civil unrest. Curfews were imposed, and Martial law was enforced and all of this led to the revolution in 1979. These were very scary times, and yet here I was working with an American aviation company within the country, Bell Helicopter. This was the closest experience I had to knowing Americans. I loved my job and these American people that I worked with. The American evacuation brought tears to everyone's eyes back then. The Americans didn't want to leave, and those of us that had come to know them, didn't want them to go. My friends were leaving and I bid them farewell, all the while remembering that my Iranian passport would keep me behind. In spite of the odds, I tried to remain optimistic.

One day in 1980, sitting on some back porch stairs, I began flipping through my phone book to call somebody for a chat, but there was nobody. They had all gone. The Shah had left the country and the Ayatollah Khomeini was now the ruling Islamic government. The thought that all my friends had left finally hit me hard. I remember telling my father that at the first opportunity I would leave the country. My father understood, and he agreed to send me to Greece, the only country that I could obtain a visa for entry.

Shortly after leaving Iran and its revolution, I developed post-traumatic stress disorder (PTSD). Sounds and mental images would remind me horrifically like movies playing in my head over and over. Sleeping was nightmarish and I would wake up claustrophobic. I was emotionally unstable and I would cry or laugh for no particular reason. I was very depressed and my physical health wasn't holding up, either. It took me six years traveling through Greece, Argentina, and Italy before finally arriving to the Great state of California in 1986. I remember that day, the day that my family, those that had all arrived here sometime before me, picked me up from the Los Angeles International airport. I can still vividly remember as we drove through Downtown L.A. because it just so happened that Bruce Springsteen was in town and the airwaves were full of his songs, and so I, too, began singing along, "Born in the USA, I was born in the USA!"

I was able to gain employment with an Aviation company in Burbank, California, and it was there that I met and married my husband. We were perfect for each other, as we shared and appreciated our musical interests. He was a drummer and played piano, and we were so much alike. There was a bond and support that

I missed in my life, and he became my security and soulmate. I learned to slowly let go of my cultural boundaries and limitations and to follow my intuition for freedom and happiness.

I had never lost hope during my darkest moments of past years despair, and now I believed that the Universe had better plans for me ahead in life.

My health situation was always a constant reminder that I needed to seek medical help at some point, and so I began visiting various doctors and specialists to address my ailments. It didn't't take long, however, before I began to feel as if I was on a roller coaster, or in a rat race here in this big city. These doctor visits were often result less, and came with tons of prescribed medications. Not only was I not feeling better, but I was getting worse. It was about that time that I learned that I had endometriosis and that there was a high probability that I would not ever bare children.

During the early '90's, California began to suffer a recession. It was the beginning of the same recession that eventually went nationwide. The job losses were tremendous during those initial years as the aviation and defense industries began to leave the state. My husband received an offer of employment in Florida, so we then relocated to Miami in 1995. It was at that point that I began thinking about music again, but on a serious level. Despite my reservations of how I thought my husband would react, I was surprised that he was not only supportive of my decision, but decided to join me in my endeavors by pursuing private piano lessons, himself. "Do what makes you happy", he said, and I was ecstatic and surprised, to say the least! This was a major turning point in my life and so we registered for music studies at the Miami Dade Wolfson Campus in Downtown Miami. Without any pre-planning, I began classical voice training for two years with Professor William Carny. At the end of each semester, to my surprise, I was selected to perform at the honor recitals by the music departments panel of jurors where I received very good reviews and encouragement to pursue my talents as an Opera singer. I didn't continue with my education, but the performance part swept me off my feet as a solo artist.

My dreams were finally coming true. The year 2000 brought about a summer when I was introduced to the King of the nightclub scene in Miami, Gerry Kelly. He was about to celebrate his big birthday bash and he envisioned putting an opera singer on stage. He asked me if I could be prepared to perform two songs in three weeks' time, and I accepted. It was a very demanding effort on the day of my audition: one that although I may have appeared calm from the outside, there was a storm churning inside of me. The voices from years passed began to haunt me as if to question whether I could actually do this or not, or if I even deserved the opportunity to be here at this moment. I realized that I had no choice but to overcome this fear and make good on my promise to the little girl that once believed in herself so long ago. It was the opportunity of a life time, and this was something that I had waited for all my life. After my audition, Mr. Kelly approached me teary eyed, congratulating me for making his night special to come. Despite me doubting how my operatic style performance would be received, he had me booked as the opening act that night, and the crowd embraced me overwhelmingly beyond my belief. The most gratifying praise that I could have ever imagined would be those with loving appreciation for the music, my performance and the show. I began to develop a following, and was offered invitations to perform at fashion shows and special events. Some of my shows were covered by local and national television channels and newspapers. My passion was to introduce modern opera to the world as a new genre, but nobody could really envision or understand my ideas at that time. I enjoyed my performances and music style nevertheless, despite being ahead of myself. Then 9/11 happened.

While I continued to carry my old chronic health issues, I also began to develop new ones, such as, anxiety attacks and muscle spasms in my chest and shoulders. I was finding them difficult to deal with, particularly with the effects of some serious narcotic medications that were casually prescribed to me by doctors. These visits would merely result in short term or failed relief efforts, and I began to lose confidence in modern western conventional medicine, so I began to do my own research for reclaiming my health. I decided to pursue a holistic lifestyle, which was something that doctors weren't prescribing.

In September of 2011, I began to experience a spherical shaped pain between my chest and back. It started within my shoulders and tightened up the muscles within my upper body. Breathing became difficult and my respiratory system slowly started to cripple. Although I sought urgent medical assistance, the relief that I was administered was merely some blood tests, X-rays, and prescriptions for anti-inflammatory and pain killers. The tests came back inconclusive with all results showing normal, and I was sent home for recovery. One doctor even commented that perhaps my condition might be within my imagination, which I found highly irritating.

Again In January of 2012, I was admitted to the hospital on an emergency basis, this time to treat a condition known as Pleural Effusion [fluid in the chest] . The symptoms were a repeat of what I had experienced back in the past. This time I was admitted for 10 days to surgically remove fluid around my left lung and chest cavity by a group of cardiology surgeons. I saw how my life was fading away before my own eyes. There were many speculations how I may have contracted this condition, but not one doctor could diagnose it specifically. It made me think about our conventional health care system and how scary and unreliable it is. By the time I left the hospital, my entire hands and arms were bruised from the many extractions of blood taken by needles, as if I were an addict of some sort. My neck veins were also routinely poked. I was physically and psychologically a wreck. I had heard of a couple of people that had died of fluid advanced to the heart cavity. I consider myself lucky to have caught my situation just in time.

My health crisis has become the turning point of my life. It took me a great length of time to gradually become healthy again. I needed to understand myself, my body, mind, and soul; and to take control. Then, one day, I encountered the Integrative Nutrition Health Coaching program, which greatly assisted me with my physical and mental ailments. It enabled me to understand that many of my conditions were accumulated over the years as a child , and that no medical professional could correctly diagnose my symptoms. In a short amount of time, I was able to relieve my joint pain, lower my excess weight, and eliminate my depression. The instruction received enabled me to understand and effect a change for the betterment of my life by eliminating my autoimmune disease and inflammation which was the cause of Pleural Effusion. What I discovered was that I had a food sensitivity to wheat and gluten since I was a child, and this was the root cause for all my suffering throughout my adult life. It was also responsible for a condition called **"Leaky Gut"**. My breakthrough into understanding my own health has been powerful enough to convince me that others enduring similar conditions could also be relieved using simple dietary techniques and gradual lifestyle changes for healing themselves.

Like many people, I used to think chronic sickness was a normal part of the human condition. Today, I know that it's simply not true. My life blossomed when I joined the Institute for Integrative Nutrition (IIN), one of the world's largest schools that teaches how to get well with Primary and Secondary Foods. The Primary Food, which is made up of four major components: exercise, spirituality, career, and relationships; and the Secondary Food, which is the food we eat. Would you be surprised as I was? The reason why the foods we eat are secondary are because they don't come close to giving us the joy, meaning, and fulfillment that primary foods provide to our hunger for love, achievement, self-expression, leadership, adventure, and spirituality. All of these elements are essential forms of nourishment to our minds.

When I learned about the concept behind healing the PERSON as a WHOLE and the basis for Bio-Individuality and understanding that each person has unique healing needs. This takes me to the next important concept IIN teaches; "one person's food can be another person's poison." It's insane to think that one dietary theory can work for all. Above and beyond all of the great things that I learned from IIN, I became my very own client to learn about, first. After years of living with autoimmune disease, I was excited to be able to reverse my symptoms slowly but progressively. Becoming a certified holistic health coach has given me a depth of desire and reward for finding my purpose. I know now that my mission is to take part in healing others in the world. It's not a secret that low quality food has a major impact in our modern society's physical and mental health. Through IIN, our concept is **preventative post-modern lifestyle.** It's essential to have a balance between primary and secondary foods in order to reach our optimal health. One can eat organic and healthy foods all day long, but if it lacks in the areas of relationship or career, life will not be balanced.

As I perfect my health coaching skills within my new career, I continue to find peace for myself as I did as a little girl in music. I enjoy performing for myself, my friends and my babies (my two large dogs), within the comfort of my home. I've learned to keep a balance in my life and having fun is a crucial part of it.

Until I realized that every cloud has a silver lining, my life seemed like a long sustained note that finally resolved into an "aha" moment. I have reached an absolute understanding and a level of GRATITUDE toward everything that I've been through. My mental and physical pains, my rejections, and my achievements in life are all instrumental in reaching harmony within myself. "Yes, I finally got it", the various stages of my life's experiences have played specific roles for the person that I am today. The Universe was preparing me for an even bigger challenge. We are in a health crisis, and my purpose now is a mission to convey a lifestyle for one's best version of themselves with a particular focus on children. Despite life's obstacles and challenges, be them unfair or unjust, life is full of beautiful colors and energy. I know that I have "arrived" and I am ready to serve.

What helped me understand my purpose in life and realizing that time is precious, were some questions that I sought answers for, especially this question stood out:

When you reach the end of your lifetime, do you think you will have any regrets, or do you think you will be able to look back and feel fully satisfied with the life that you had lived?

Imagine, just by adapting small sustainable changes, such as, thinking positive, adding physical activities that I love, and making the right choices of food for myself; I'm emotionally stable, clear and focused. Today, I am an unshakable optimist who believes in changing the world for a better place. My personal goal is to live, enjoy, and serve every day as though each day is the last day of my life. I am a dream builder enduring a journey, with trust in the Universe as my guide through the next STAGE of my OPERA.

I was introduced to Napoleon Hill by my publisher Debbie Horovitch. Napoleon Hill has mentioned in his dynamic book titled Think and Grow Rich, How to Get Dreams Off the Launching-Pad, he states, '*A burning desire to be and to do is the starting point from which the dreamer must take off. Dreams are not born of indifference, laziness, or lack of ambition. Remember that all who succeed in life get off to a bad start, and pass through many heartbreaking struggles before they "arrive". The turning point in the lives of those who succeed usually comes at the moment of some crisis, through which they are introduced to their "other selves."*'

I know today that love and support have tremendous healing powers in whom we are and become. It is an unstoppable force in whatever we desire to do. I have found my voice and a career helping people become the person they most want to be, while I continue to heal myself, too.

My special thanks and appreciation to my husband. Although I possessed quality attributes within me, he is my drive and support. His role in who I have become today, is the basis for my life story. Without him I would not be participating in this book. The power of his mind, strong will, and belief have been impressive to me throughout our lives together of 26 years. He is the wings that have empowered me to fly. I dedicate this book to my beloved husband, James Cuellar.

About Persia Cuellar

Persia Cuellar is an Entrepreneur, Classical Singer, Short Filmmaker, Natural Chef, and a Certified Integrative Nutrition Health Coach.

She has graduated from the Institute for Integrative Nutrition and is the Founder of **New Gen Lifestyle**. After years of struggling health and almost a near death experience, she decided to claim her own health by taking matters into her own hands. Becoming a health coach has enabled her to heal herself through self-experimentation.

She discovered that her years of substandard health were linked to **LEAKY GUT SYNDROME.** Since then, it's been her obsession to pursue her better health which in turn has fueled her passion to assist and educate others whom may also have **LEAKY GUT,** and may not even know it. She practices virtual one-on-one coaching and offers groups sessions.

The father of modern medicine *Hippocrates* said **"All disease begins in the Gut"** and research is now proven he was absolutely right.

Her specialty is in addressing **LEAKY GUT** syndrome and the symptoms associated with it, are: bloating, food sensitivities, thyroid conditions, fatigue, joint pain, headaches, skin issues, digestive problems, weight gain, and depression. What causes Leaky Gut? Poor diet, chronic stress, toxin overload, and bacterial imbalance.

Website:	http://www.newgenlifestyle.com/
Email:	info@persiacuellar.com
Facebook:	http://facebook.com/persiacuellar
Twitter:	twitter.com/cuellarpersia
Location:	Miami, Florida, USA

Self-Acceptance

The Wandering Years
By Kathy Jalali

> *"I wish I could show you,*
> *when you are lonely or in the darkness,*
> *the astonishing light of your own being"*
> *- Hafiz*

2016 started with the intention of "making peace with the past." Our past is good for two things: to learn from and to enjoy. I spent most of my time "learning" and, eventually, there came a time to "enjoy" the memories and reframe my narrative. My quest sent me off to two different parts of the world—Iran and Sweden—where I had spent turbulent stages of my childhood and adolescent life. Revisiting the past with my two young daughters and husband was overwhelmingly emotional and empowering. The vibrant smell of spices in the bazaar, the magnificent clouds in the Scandinavian horizon, old friends and back alleys of familiar neighborhoods were all bittersweet and nostalgic hints of a distant lifetime. They were reminders of happiness, loneliness, struggles, and, ultimately, a search for truth. I realized that the underlying motive for this mission was to tell my story—an act of transcending the personal and bringing order to my universe by making it clearer how I see the world and my role within it.

I was born in Iran in the mid-seventies and, by the time I was seven, I had lived in the United States twice and witnessed a revolution and the eruption of a bloody war. Memories of my first day of elementary school in Iran are vague, but the powerful explosive blasts have since been etched on my memory. The days that followed included panic, air raid sirens, loss of electricity, rations, and long queues. Life became unpredictable and gloomy, and yet I was young and oblivious. Surrounded by a loving family and friends, the tragedies of war were somewhat beyond the scope of my innocent world. Little did I know that the winds of war would eventually blow our way and affect me and millions of others who would become part of the Iranian diaspora.

By the time I was twelve, we had adapted to a new a norm and uncertainty was woven into the fabric of our lives. While the majority of the war took place at the battlefront by the borders, there were also frequent strikes directed towards the civilians. After each explosion, I was paralyzed with anxiety and dreaded the extent of the destruction and human casualties. The heartbreak dampened our spirits, but also taught us survival and resilience. Five years into the war, my parents were still determined to stay in Iran, hoping for the light at the end of the tunnel. Their decision changed on the day my elementary school became the target for another explosion.

I remember the day quite vividly. I was taking a math test and suddenly the air raid siren blasted. The thunderous sound of the fighter jets elevated into a crescendo, followed by ear-shattering explosions and an eruption of panic. The school shook as if hit by a powerful earthquake, and everyone started running towards the door. I got crushed beneath the larger bodies and by the time I was able to get out, my whole face was covered in blood. It had been a close call—the site of the explosion was a couple of blocks from the school. The anxiety that followed the attack affected me both physically and mentally for years. I was hospitalized for an acute body rash and became sensitive to loud noises. For my family, the danger was suddenly tangible, and it was time to leave Iran.

Our attempts for obtaining visas to a once-familiar home in the United States were denied and, eventually, we planned to settle in Sweden where my uncle and his family resided. Bidding farewell to my relatives and friends and wondering whether I would ever see them again was agonizing. As I said goodbye to my room and the weeping willow in the backyard, I felt vulnerable and helpless. Fearing the unknown, I vowed to myself to quickly regain control over my destiny; therefore, an incessant need for control became an exhausting part of my life. My mother, younger brothers and I left Iran, and my father planned to join us shortly after—but he ended up being delayed for almost two years. His frequent long letters became my only comfort and the means of connecting with the past.

I was no stranger to international moves, and yet relocating to a homogeneously populated small town in Sweden proved to be challenging—and very lonely. As I walked out in the streets for the first time, I was faced with a new reality: as a short and dark brunette with big curly hair and a thick unibrow, I clearly stood out like a sore thumb. When I finally started school, I was confronted with pity and indifference—it felt like I was invisible. I realized that proving my very existence would be my main struggle. I started to question my identity and became self-conscious of my looks and heritage. The once-playful girl in me was becoming withdrawn and isolated. I escaped, through books and classical music, to my imaginary happy place in which I experienced peace and calmness.

There was no time for my emotional struggles. My younger brothers were frequently bullied, verbally and physically. Our immigration process was denied, and we were faced with the possibility of an immediate deportation. My mother was overwhelmed and emotionally drained, and I became involved with the everyday decisions, assuming partial parenting responsibilities for my younger brothers. Barely a teen, I was on a fast track to adulthood. A nearby lake became my hiding place where I would spend my time reading books and listening to music. As I became more withdrawn, I started having anxiety attacks and frequent fainting episodes. After extensive medical investigation, I was told that that my symptoms were likely a coping mechanism in response to stress and previous trauma.

After nearly two years, the day came when my father was finally reunited with us. It was the happiest moment since we had moved to Sweden. We were once again a family and some level of normalcy returned our lives. I started high school and gradually started to feel more integrated and at ease with the Swedish way of life. I started to develop friendships, and my physical and mental health began to improve. Despite our overall progress in fitting in, my parents were concerned about future career prospects and making ends meet and as soon as we were able to secure our immigration status to Canada, they decided to migrate again. Once again, my world and sense of stability were shattered.

Our journey continued on a different continent. We moved to Canada and, eventually, to the United States. Along the way, we made memories and friends, which were ultimately left behind. The sequence of emotions was the same—loss, grief and the quest for new, meaningful relationships. War and diaspora were the consistent integral element of our identities. When the time came for me to choose a career path, I was at a crossroads. Torn between obligation and inspiration, I was reminded that having a higher education was not merely a source of pride for me, but also for my family as a whole. It was time to regain control over my life, but the weight of family expectations was heavy on my shoulders; unfortunately, there was no time for creativity and exploration. Upon completing a graduate degree in engineering, I landed a job as a scientist in the corporate world. Over the years, my career progressed, yet I was perpetually unfulfilled. I questioned my credentials and capabilities and, finally, decided to pursue a part-time MBA. Nonetheless, my restlessness lingered.

My self-discovery pursuit also took its toll on my personal relationships. Mastering the perpetual practice of detachment, I was emotionally guarded and not ready for commitments nor starting a family. In spite of my calm and composed facade, I was anxious and in need of a meaningful connection. My frequent nightmares of the war and the recurrence of my fainting episodes were clearly indications of an internal chaos, but I refused to confide in anyone or seek professional help. I was determined to stay tough and figure things out on my own. Despite the emotional exhaustion, I was not ready to resolve my feelings and, instead, sought instant gratification and distractions. Ironically, my creative expression, self-integration and renewal of joy was inspired by the exhilaration from travel and change. It was during this time that I met my husband, who happened to live across the country. Apparently, I was destined to move again.

By this time, I was convinced that academic and career achievements were not necessarily the pathway to happiness. So, in pursuit of love, I left my career and immediate family, who had been an integral part of my life, and relocated to Washington, DC. Fortunately, my husband was very loving and supportive and encouraged me to pursue the path to find my purpose. My mind was fixated on happiness as an end goal and I was unsure how to proceed. The idea of an honest and complete reinvention of myself felt like a betrayal to my past and to my hard-earned education. I also feared defeat and failure. My love-hate relationship with change was hitting a brick wall, and I realized that my ambivalence made me dependent on control and a sense of unattainable order. I needed to give myself permission to "let go.

Motherhood had been a long-term vision, and I had assumed that it would occur as a consequence of a happy relationship. I was in my mid-thirties and, since my life purpose had not been revealed, in search for answers, I turned to parenthood. Blessed with two daughters in a span of three years, I noticed the glimmers of hope confirming my own being. Having my girls was a life-altering experience, and I discovered a wide spectrum of emotions—emotions that had been dormant since childhood. I was given a chance to see things anew through my daughters' eyes. Motherhood was like walking around with all of my nerve endings raw and exposed. I was starting to experience the full measure of being alive. My emotional system was rebooting and motherhood had indeed served its purpose in opening my eyes and helping me appreciate the most wonderful wonders of the world.

Despite being a pragmatic scientist most of my life, I started to believe that "not everything" is random. While motherhood helped create in me an awareness of my environment and provided a mirror for me to see the reflection of my inner soul, I also rediscovered yoga. My journey with yoga began as an alternative way to exercise and work out. As I practiced more regularly, my body started to move in new ways and shift into new positions. The poses stirred up the old stories from the past and encouraged me to face my challenges with a new perspective. As I was told repeatedly, I concentrated on the breath. It was frustrating in the beginning, but I learned to build more awareness and focus my attention. For the first time in my life, I found a safe and non-judgmental space that made me feel grounded; it reminded me of another safe place—the lake in Sweden. Yoga had a way of making the seemingly imperfect pieces of my life beautiful. Life was simply a practice; none of it was beautiful and all of it was beautiful!

As I developed a yoga practice, I further recognized the imbalances in my body, the duality of my mind, and the ongoing void in my relationships, with a kinder and more accepting attitude. I became aware that I needed to give myself permission to finally "trust," "settle" and "surrender." I decided to enroll in a yoga teacher training program, which I completed as I turned forty. I felt empowered by having genuinely followed my own will for the very first time. A couple of retreats later, I gradually connected with my once non-existent spirituality and appreciated the intelligence of the universal consciousness. This encounter with mystery was accompanied by a deep sense of awe and wonder, followed by an immense feeling of humility. As a scientist, I was fully aware of this dichotomy but, to my great surprise, I felt comfortable and at ease.

During this time, I developed a wrist injury that prompted me to focus on my physical health in a different way. I became interested in integrated health and nutrition and immediately signed up for the Health Coach Certification program through the Institute of Integrative Nutrition. I learned that our purpose is ever-evolving and, in order to claim our purpose, we have to realize it on a daily basis. During the certification process, I frequently reflected on my childhood and felt liberated in accepting what I was not able to change. As a recovering perfectionist, I developed a love for mind-body balance and wellness and knew that my life purpose had gradually revealed itself. It was time for me to share what I had learned with my family, friends and millions of like-minded people.

In telling the story of how we became who we are and of who we are on our way to becoming, the story itself becomes a part of our essence. In order to discover the silver lining, we need to acknowledge the past, cherish the present, and hope for the future. My greatest revelations and growth were achieved in my valleys rather than my mountaintops. The sum of all my experiences that have shaped resilience, empathy, compassion and, ultimately, truth, are the silver lining in my story. And, although my story is unfinished, there is gratitude, presence and peace. As I take a break from writing, I hear my girls singing: "I'm growing up – way, way up - I'm growing up with hopes and dreams - making my way into the world." And my heart bursts with joy and love and I appreciate the privilege of life.

About Kathy Jalali

Kathy is a Certified Health and Lifestyle Coach and the founder of **"Happy Cinnamon."**

She helps busy individuals create simple and effective lifestyle practices that improve their overall state of wellbeing.

A traveling yogi, Kathy's 10 years of experience in the corporate world combined with a unique blend of art, science, culture, food and music have developed her self-expression in exploring mind-body connection. She believes that a combination of the best of ancient wisdom and modern science provides the most effective path to optimal health, peak performance and, ultimately, happiness.

Kathy has degrees in Microbiology and Biochemical Engineering from the University of British Columbia, Canada, and a MBA from the University of California, Irvine. She is also a graduate of the Institute for Integrative Nutrition and is a Certified Yoga Instructor. Kathy provides coaching services, creating customized strategies for those who are seeking life balance and better health.

Kathy resides in Washington, DC, with her husband and two daughters. She enjoys traveling, watching her children laugh and play together, and breathing deeply as often as possible.

Website: http://www.HappyCinnamon.com
Facebook: https://www.facebook.com/spiceupyourwellness/
Instagram: https://www.instagram.com/spiceupyourwellness/
LinkedIn: https://www.linkedin.com/in/kathyjalali

Where Does Wellness Begin?
By Angela Sidlo

I sat on the couch, feverishly working my way to the bottom of a pint of Ben & Jerry's ice cream, a nightly ritual for me after a twelve-hour day running my own restaurant. I was in my mid-thirties, oblivious to the fact that my adrenals were completely exhausted, my gut health was tanking and I was on the verge of a crash. That pint of ice cream was my escape. It told me I did a good job today, it comforted me, it gave me the sweetness that I was missing in my life. It didn't ask me if I paid the payroll taxes on time or nag at me to sign the contract for the next gourmet food show. It was there every night, waiting for me with its creamy delicious chunks of chocolate and frozen cherries, like little rewards.

My road to wellness began nearly two decades ago. Back then, if someone would have told me a donkey, an Italian restaurant and a wonderful counselor would be the catalyst for change in my journey to wellness, I would have told them they were completely nuts. Let me share with you how it all unfolded.

My grandparents played a strong influence in my formative years. We lived across the lane from them until I was eleven and then less than half of a mile away. Grandma taught me to play piano, let me use her treadle sewing machine and taught me to make perfect pasta. She was kind and patient and generous with hugs and kisses. She grew the most beautiful roses in her garden and had a real eye for style.

Grandpa was the mayor of the rural town I grew up in and owned the grocery store. He taught me that hard work and honesty would take me far in life. That was true, but I had really overdone the hard work part and failed at being really honest about taking care of my financial health as well as my physical health.

My grandfather served as my informal business advisor up until the time he passed away. He often warned me of doing too much. I should have listened more to that advice, but I was determined to be somebody. Over the years, I have learned to shift from a place of self-destruction to a place of self-care. It is not easy, but it begins with my daily mantra, "Taking care of myself allows me to be fully present and help others do the same." It has been an invaluable tool for me in the healing process.

The rest of my family was very dysfunctional. My father was an alcoholic and the local barber in town. I'm pretty sure that for every haircut, he walked across the street to the bar and drank a beer. If my grandparents hadn't owned a grocery store, I wonder if we would have gone hungry many times. As a teenager, I remember putting part of my waitressing pay check toward the family budget.

My mother was a homemaker. She dabbled in get rich quick schemes that usually cost more money than she made. As kids, my brother, sister and I sold paring knives, furniture polish, fire extinguishers and stain-remover as her sales minions. The fighting and violence at home made any hope of normal family life non-existent. I could never have friends over to spend the night for fear my dad would come home drunk and make a scene. My mother coped by yelling a lot and physically abusing my brother. I suspect she too suffered from hormonal imbalances. My mother and father did the best they could, but I was forced to grow up way too quickly.

They separated the summer I turned seventeen. My brother stayed with my father and my sister, foster brother and I went with mother. The fall after their separation, I dropped out of my senior year in high school to get married. My husband, who was 19, had just joined the Coast Guard. New Orleans was our first duty station, 1,200 miles from the chaos of an alcoholic family. I thought I was safe. Little did I know just how much emotional baggage I had brought with me, baggage that eventually manifested as dis-ease in my body.

Within the year I was a new mother myself. I was only 18 and very determined to never make the mistakes my parents made in raising me. I worked hard to get my GED before my other classmates back home graduated from high school. Leaving the only town I had ever known as home, being away from my friends, cousins and my grandparents was hard. I would experience periods of deep sadness but didn't know it was the beginnings of depression.

My husband and I had another child two years later and then transferred to Oregon. We did three more years in the Coast Guard before deciding to settle down and raise our sons on the Oregon coast. I took classes at the local community college and taught preschool at the YMCA and my husband got his Associate degree. He soon got a job with UPS as a driver.

After becoming the first in my family to get an Associate degree, I worked for the school district as an instructional assistant and waitressed in the summers. I longed for the pasta my grandmother and I used to make so I started making flavored pastas at home. I took them to school to share with coworkers. Everyone loved it and Premier Pasta was born. I bought a commercial pasta machine, set it up in the back of the restaurant I worked at during the summer months and began selling product to local restaurants and at the farmers' market. Juggling two active boys, a full-time job and a growing business began to wear on me. I wasn't getting enough sleep and I was eating on the fly most of the time. I thought I could do it all. After all, my family background taught me to be a very strong-willed, independent woman.

I left the school district job to dive head-first into the pasta business, traveling to California to purchase more machines to make more pasta. At our peak, the business produced 23,000 pounds of pasta in one year. There were gourmet food shows, restaurant deliveries, cooking classes, winemakers dinners, a cookbook and a restaurant serving lunch and dinner six days a week.

Obviously, there were too many balls in the air at one time. My day consisted of a whirlwind: getting the boys off to school, heading to the shop for my first espresso of the day and taking down the pasta from the drying racks that we made the previous day, getting the soup of the day started, running to United Grocers for supplies, opening for lunch at eleven, making the pasta run, doing the books and bank deposit and gearing up for the dinner crowd. It was a recipe for disaster and only a matter of time before the pot boiled over.

I had this underlying need or drive or crazy thought that I had to do all of this to prove something. I didn't know what. I was creating the same chaos with this business that I had come from in my dysfunctional upbringing. Underneath I knew it, but I seemed destined to ride this train to the end of the tracks, full speed ahead!

In later years, through therapy, I would discover a crucial link that I had recreated the same chaos and dysfunction in my business I had grown up with in my family. I felt a sense of separateness that kept me from being in the flow of life. Asking for help was so hard because I was never taught how. I had always been in survival mode from the time I was a toddler. Dwelling on past experiences had become my current reality.

Both of my sons graduated from high school and went on to lead wonderful lives. One moved to Hawaii and the other one joined the Coast Guard. My husband and I felt proud that we raised two beautiful children. Meanwhile, the business was failing. I was $40,000 in debt. Sleep was elusive and interrupted constantly with panic attacks. My moodiness was getting worse and my joints ached all the time. I was so bitchy no one wanted to be around me. I felt old and worn out, trapped in a body full of emotion and pain, ready to explode. I decided to see my doctor and was diagnosed with fibromyalgia, perimenopause, arthritis and depression.

These diagnoses are the way that Western medicine categorizes symptoms. I felt fibromyalgia was a label. It seemed to me, in the 90's most doctors used this diagnosis when they really didn't know what is wrong with you. Up until this time in my life, I had been a healthy, physically active, bright, hard-working young woman, determined to do something worthwhile with my life. At that point, I was just sick and tired of being sick and tired.

The cravings for carbs and sugar had been increasing and my energy levels plummeting, but I didn't put two and two together. I was too tired to think beyond the here and now of getting through the day. At the time, I hadn't made the connection between food and mood or how it related to hormones. Later I would learn that food cravings have a deep root in hormonal imbalances. When estrogen, insulin and leptin are out of balance you crave carb-laden, sugary foods like a starved prisoner.

After being diagnosed, the decision was made to sell the wholesale pasta manufacturing to a company that I had been doing private labeling for. I closed the restaurant and it felt like I had failed, let myself down. Closing the business closed down a part of me. I went to work at a traditional desk job for the next four years, where I put on twenty pounds and continued to experience depression, anxiety, anger, joint pain and poor sleep. A desk job, for me, was like trying to put a square peg in a round hole. It just didn't work. I felt trapped in my body, trapped in my job and longing to do something of importance with my life, but I had no energy. I felt numb and disconnected.

I fumbled through a myriad of prescription drugs including Paxil, Amitriptyline, Celebrex and the list goes on. They made my weight gain worse, left me feeling lethargic most of the day and sent me deeper into mood swings and depression. My eating habits were still poor and I continued to binge on sugar and carbs.

Each morning was a struggle to get out of bed. I just wanted to pull the covers over my head and shut the world out. Caffeine was my method of self-medication in the morning and then again mid-afternoon to bring my energy levels back up.

This was a false sense of energy that I was giving my body, which continued the cycle of hormonal imbalance. It was obvious that I had been under a lot of stress from the previous demands of running a business and caffeine had hijacked my adrenals, putting my cortisol levels dangerously in flux. The imbalance in the microflora of my gut had disrupted my serotonin levels and caused depression, mood swings and panic attacks. Ultimately the diagnosis was related to my lifestyle and work schedule. My body had constantly tried to keep up with my racing mind, compromising the body systems in the attempt. The crash had been inevitable.

From the outside, the world saw me as a typical woman, now in her forties, with a loving husband, two wonderful sons, living in one of the most beautiful places on earth with enough money to live comfortably. Inside I felt hollow, lifeless, as though my light had faded away. I was still looking for the sweetness in life that I felt was missing. I fought to find the answers to the underlying cause of my illness and reclaim a vibrant life, full of possibilities and opportunities.

Overlooking the commitment to take care of myself and put my health first, I overextended myself once again with an additional job.

My depression wasn't improving. I would have devastating lows paired with euphoric highs. I worried I was going crazy. I even went to a counselor for a mental assessment, but still had no answers from Western medicine. I was going to counseling, but felt that it was only helping on the surface, I wasn't getting to the root of this thing that had such a hold on me. I cycled through at least a dozen therapists, trying to find the right one who understood me and could offer some help.

One counselor was exceptional, however. Jackie was known for her work in hypnotherapy. She took me through a series of guided meditations in our sessions where I was able to go back to those old childhood hurts surrounding alcoholism and the turbulence of my home situation. She held that sacred space for me where healing begins to happen. She allowed me to see the anger, fear and uncertainty of that child within me. The inner child that had to grow up so quickly, that child who felt overachieving would somehow soothe her, make her feel good enough. The psychotherapy was a key tool for me to begin to understand how to redesign my life without having to feel compelled to do it all as a means to fill the void.

A few nights after one of my sessions with her I had a pivotal dream. It was the first glimmer of hope and helped set my course to wellness. In the dream, I found myself deep in a cavern. It was cold and damp and I had lost my way. As I felt my way down one of the cramped, claustrophobic tunnels, it suddenly opened up into a domed room. In the middle of the room was a small wooden table. There, a woman was sitting in a chair at the table with a scarf over her head and face. She motioned for me to come closer. I explained to her I was lost and asked if she knew the way out. She pointed to the far side of the room and at the top of the wall there was light coming in. She said it was the way out. I crawled up to the ledge and moved the foliage aside to see a narrow opening big enough for me to crawl out. I turned back to thank the woman and as I looked back she had removed her scarf to reveal herself. She was the reflection of me. I was looking back at myself, a wiser more mature self. She said, "Don't forget to come back and visit. You are always welcome here". I couldn't believe what I was seeing! I stared in amazement.

A sense of calm came over me, a peace that I had never experienced before. When I awoke from the dream I realized my ability to heal was within me. I truly knew the way out, the way to better health from the inside out. From that day forward I started to change the way I thought about illness. I wasn't a victim of fibromyalgia or hormone imbalance or depression. I had the ability to figure this out. I just had to look at it differently. Changing the way I looked at things gave me the ability to feel compassion and understanding for myself and begin to know the healer within.

For nearly two decades' hormonal imbalances created lows that were the worst. It made me binge on carbs, ravenously craving French fries, cookies and ice cream. I could eat a whole package of cookies within an hour. Then I would rebound from bingeing to total self-loathing and negative self-talk. I had been indulging in negative food behaviors and poor relationship choices as a coping mechanism for many years until I had a donkey named Annie and everything began to unfold in divine order.

As a child, summers were spent with my other Grandma in the Nebraska sand hills. Oh, I loved that place, with all the animals, a big victory garden and the peach tree. We used to pick peaches from the tree and hold a bowl of fresh cut peaches under the milk separator and watch the fresh cream drizzle over the juicy ripe fruit. What a treat! I was happy then and I thought I would be happy again if I could feel that contentment that I did back then.

I knew that I wanted more than a desk job in life, I was destined for more than that. So my husband and I bought eight acres on the Oregon coast after our boys left home. We filled the farm with horses, mules, donkeys, cats, dogs, chickens, cows, turkeys and pheasants, and even raised two pigs. The farm reminded me of my dad's mother, strong, independent and resourceful.

Annie was my biggest donkey. She stood sixteen hands tall, taller than my husband's horse. We affectionately referred to her as a Donkasaurus. Annie had an autoimmune disease that caused fluid to collect in her joints, making life painful for her. We tried to manage it with medication, with little success.

The Oregon State University veterinary school did a myriad of tests on her, but they couldn't figure it out either. I began to look for alternative ways to treat her. One day, I was in the local herb shop exploring devil's claw and arnica as pain relievers for her when I saw a flyer for reiki. I had never heard of it, but it is a form of energy work that could relieve pain, so I called the number on the brochure. I asked the woman if she had ever done reiki on a donkey before. She was a bit surprised but agreed to try. At this point, Annie was lying down at least fourteen hours a day, which compromises circulation and internal organ function.

Mary was a reiki practitioner and came to do a session on Annie. It seemed harmless. She placed her hands on Annie. Annie seemed to relax and enjoy the attention. The next day Annie was up and active and the next few days after that, so I decided there must be something to this reiki technique. A few months later, I took my first reiki class. When the instructor wrote the reiki symbols out on the board in the classroom I nearly fell out of my seat. They were the same symbols that I used to draw over and over in my sketch books as a child. The pieces were starting to fall into place and I knew I was on the right track.

It was good to work on Annie every day and see her improve. Annie loved Mary's visits and she ambled across the field to greet her each time. On one of her visits, we were celebrating a warm summer day with wine glasses full of Sangria. Annie came up behind Mary, stretched her neck over her shoulder, plunked her big floppy donkey lips into her wine glass and sucked down the entire Sangria. She licked her lips and ambled back out to the field, leaving us laughing hysterically!

One of the practices new reiki students adopt is to run reiki on ourselves every day for the first forty-five days of our training. Like a good student, I followed my master's instruction and also gave reiki to Annie every day. It was wonderful to see her improve, but the biggest revelation came when one day as I was scooping barn stalls and realized I wasn't so sad anymore. I was feeling better, I felt alive with energy. I couldn't help but think, "Wow! This really works!!"

My love of plant medicine was insatiable. The garden was always full of interesting herbs and vegetables. Each time I moved, I would dig up my favorites and take with me like they were furniture that couldn't be left behind. I have medicinal herbs that I started over twenty years ago that are still with me today. I had played around with essential oils before but got more serious with them in my reiki practice. I knew they possessed healing qualities. Soon I was enrolled in JennScents Institute, an aromatherapy school to become adept as an aromatherapist. Essential oils work to heal the body on an emotional and physical level and I could feel the benefits of less joint and muscle pain and a more even emotional disposition.

Being the entrepreneur my grandfather taught me to be, I opened up a little shop in town and offered reiki and aromatherapy to others. One day, one of my reiki friends invited me to go to a tai chi class, so we ventured out together. The instructor approached me afterwards and suggested that I become a teacher. I enjoyed the gentle moves and it helped my joints feel less painful. Soon I took the training and was teaching tai chi weekly. Later, I was awarded two grants to teach tai chi countywide. I was beginning to see that as I was healing, I had enough energy to help others heal.

Reiki, aromatherapy and tai chi made a marked difference in my wellbeing. I was getting better sleep, my moods were stabilizing, and I felt an inner peace that I had long been disconnected from. Instead of all the heavy Italian foods I sought comfort in, I started exploring stir-fry, dark green leafy veggies and eating less sugar, carbs and caffeine.

Soon after that, I enrolled in the Seattle Reflexology & Massage Center program and to become a certified reflexologist. Getting the body realigned energetically was the first step toward wellness for me. Aromatherapy and reflexology calmed the nervous system and offered aid to all my other body systems, initiating the next step towards wellness. Learning how to balance my life physically, mentally and emotionally through the practice of tai chi made it possible to continue to embrace wellness. I was well on my way to a happier healthier life and wanted to help others to do the same.

Through the health coach program and Joshua Rosenthal at the Institute for Integrative Nutrition, I learned the importance of taking care of all the things in your life that nourish you that you don't find on your plate. Spirituality, relationships, physical activity and career all feed you in ways that food can't. Finding balance in those areas will change the foods that you choose to put on your plate and nourish your body. Following this strategy, I have created a toolbox of modalities to share with others to help them explore what imbalances they may be experiencing and work together to have that happy healthy life once again. I share deep gratitude to my loving husband, family, animals, counselors, teachers and friends for helping me on my journey to wellness.

Today, I am teaching healthy, anti-inflammatory cooking classes at the local community college where, twenty years ago I taught Italian cooking classes filled with carb heavy, sugar laden, and hormone disrupting foods. A plant-based diet full of nutrient dense foods has been one of the key components to hormone balancing and mood management for me in my journey to better health. The health of the gut is a vital key to a healthy brain. This is a subject that western medicine receives no training in and where health coaches fill the gaps for those who want to experience true wellness.

We cannot treat imbalances in the body by treating individual symptoms. In my holistic health business today I treat my clients like plants. I want to know about the soil they are growing in, looking at the biological terrain to see the whole person and give aid from there. I believe that my symptoms presented as a lack of balance in my life that began in childhood and manifested as disease.

Stress played a major part in my illness. As a society, we use the word stress so frequently it has lost its meaning. Finding ways to manage stress has become a major focus in my life. Spending time in nature, taking Epsom salt baths with essential oils, doing tai chi on the beach and finding time to unplug from social media and television have become key components in my stress management.

Luckily, I was able to have a very loving and supportive husband, a thirst for learning and magical opportunities to see the silver lining in the lessons I was given and share that wisdom with my clients who suffer from depression, fibromyalgia, hormonal imbalances and weight gain. The pint of ice cream I eat from now is filled with spiritual food, physical activity, healthy relationships and a fantastic career helping people to be well. I share my wisdom in hopes that you can find balance and health to live the life of your dreams too.

Today, I am an author, teacher, public speaker and Holistic Aromatherapist who serves as the Oregon director for the National Association for Holistic Aromatherapists. I am also a Usui Reiki Master Teacher, Tai Chi Instructor, Certified Reflexologist and an Integrative Nutrition Certified Health Coach with a healthy holistic practice on the Oregon coast.

About Angela Sidlo

Angela Sidlo is a holistic health practitioner. She has been involved in health and wellness for over 20 years, honing her skills as a certified health coach, reflexologist, aromatherapist, reiki master teacher and tai chi instructor. This toolbox of modalities allows Angela to joyfully assist others find true wellness so they can move forward to live life to the fullest.

Angela works one-on-one with clients or in group settings (in-person or online) to help those who struggle with weight loss, hormone imbalance, depression and fibromyalgia.

If you would like to connect with Angela and her work, go to www.AngelaSidlo.com

Email: http://angela.sidlo@gmail.com
Facebook: https://www.facebook.com/angela.sidlo
Instagram: aromatherapyworks
Location: Astoria, Oregon

Awakening Through Fear
by Lisa Laura

Fear: My Comfort Blanket

Throughout most of my adult life, I thought I was living life on my terms. I was dealing with life's challenges the best way I knew how. What I didn't realize then, is that I was doing more harm to myself than good. Coming from a place of love instead of fear has changed my life so much that I could never go back to the way I was. It has changed my world and it has changed me. I am now the best version of me.

I suppressed my emotions because I didn't know how to address them constructively. Divorce, loss, and isolation have been strong influences in my life and have impacted my emotional behavior and emotional responses. I used to cover up and avoid my feelings with alcohol and food. I also used my relationships as an escape, to not deal with what I needed to confront. Then one day I realized that if it was to be better—it was up to me. I was the only person who could change my life.

I was miserable and unhappy yes—but my life was familiar—so I suffered in silence. I was trapped in an uncomfortable comfort zone. Change demands acceptance—and it is not easy. It requires courage to face your fears and choose an unfamiliar path. I chose to be brave and I have become my own inspiration. I hope that sharing my story will inspire others also.

It starts with awareness

I've learned that life isn't so black and white and that it's more about living comfortably in the discomfort, which is the grey area. I did find however, that life became much clearer when I decided to make room for growth and drop anything that was keeping me stuck.

This was after I decided to go AWOL for a while. I was consumed by anxiety, anger and a lack of clarity. I was overwhelmed by sadness. I then discovered that these were all deeply rooted in fear.

I have always considered myself to be a "glass half full" kind of person. But now I needed to take control of my life. I was the one with the power to make a change. I needed to heal myself from the inside out. Taking a vacation, a new romance or finding a new job, were not the answer. The solution lay within. I needed to not only change my behavior but also my mental attitude. I started to realize what it meant to be a human-being instead of a human-doing.

Time to put me first

I checked in often and started to put myself first. This meant establishing daily rituals that felt good to me like learning to slow down, journaling more, creating more, and getting back to the activities that filled me with joy. I became aware of my thought processes and found them to be negatively influenced so I created routines around mindset. These include meditation, breath work, establishing new beliefs, and creating my perfect life vision. One practice I hold close is around how I want to feel. Because I had fear instilled in me from a very young age, I had to unlearn my 'go to' reactions. It's been a challenge, since as a child I watched horror movies as a way of bonding with my family. These movies terrified yet thrilled me but I cherished these moments because they brought me comfort. My life has been a similar story—I constantly lived life on the edge of my seat. It may sound strange, but fear has been my security blanket.

I have found that my relationships have been created through fear. I have become attached to people, situations and outcomes that weren't always right for me. I settled and sacrificed my truth to spare other people's feelings and also to avoid being alone. I had to learn to be okay with change, because it is inevitable. I struggled a lot with self-acceptance and self-worth. With all of this, I prevailed, I kept going.

Fear has been my biggest motivator. It constantly pushed me. It always left me searching for my next adventure. Though living my life completely terrified, there hasn't been a moment that I let fear stop me from accomplishing a single thing I wanted to do. As much as fear was my worst enemy, it also became a familiar friend.

Striving for Balance

I have always been that go-to person for people. In my family, among my friends and at work, people would naturally open up to me. For the most part, I would just listen. Then I would reflect back to them what they were saying in a way that shed new light on their situation and that ultimately shifted their perspective. I came by this gift by living honestly.

I owe a lot of this insight to the ones who raised me. My parents were on completely opposite ends of the emotional spectrum. My experiences as a child, provided insight and an ability as an adult, to find balance between extremes when it comes offering perspective and the processing of emotions.

Growing up, my mother tended to be negative, fearful, depressed and at times overly-dramatic. She is a caring and compassionate woman and would do anything for those she loves, but she has always had a hard time seeing the bright side of life. I was raised in this somber atmosphere, unaware of the effects this mindset had on me.

My dad, on the other hand, is the complete opposite. We spent every Saturday together and I consider him my best friend. He was always high on life and looking on the bright side of things. He disliked confrontation and often let things slide of his back, so to speak, rather than deal with unpleasant or difficult situations. I now realize he is sometimes too passive and unwilling to process uncomfortable emotions.

Balancing myself between these two diverse personalities has given me a gift. I am able to help others find middle ground with their emotions–and I am grateful for this unique ability. What I didn't realize was that when it came to my own emotions I was completely lost.

It was as though I was a "special blend" of emotions. I was either so intense that I could barely contain myself or I was void of emotion. Balance was non-existent.

I began to notice patterns in my behaviour—what set me off—how I dealt with confrontation.

When it came to situations that I couldn't control, I was a mess. My emotions went wild. I acted like a toddler when I didn't get what I wanted. I had the emotional intelligence of a two year old. I was emulating learned behavior. My mother had been a drama queen and I simply did not know any better.

When it came to confrontation, I stuck my head in the sand. I wanted no part of it. I often kept my opinions to myself and when confronted with conflict I would take the easy way out and side with things I disagreed with just to keep the peace. My self-esteem and self-confidence suffered. I no longer had a voice.

I knew that the behavior of today was rooted in my past—so I started digging.

I was three years old when my parents got a divorce. Although I don't remember that period in great detail, it had a tremendous impact on me and naturally my experiences, shaped who I am today.

Following the divorce, I suffered from separation anxiety. I hated being alone and feared being apart from those I loved even more so. Life was short and fear of loss controlled my behavior. I didn't know how to be alone with myself or my thoughts and I had no desire to learn.

This attitude—this fear—resulted in my attaching myself to whatever and whoever was available. Not the healthiest reason to be in a relationship. I have since learned that it is truly important to be whole as an individual and not to rely on others to complete you.

My mother never fully recovered from the divorce. I lived with her and watched the hurt and the pain become depression. Without even realizing it—I was instilled with the belief that relationships caused pain and suffering.

My mom is an amazing woman, my biggest fan. She is very strong, but she doesn't see that. Her will to truly live has never surpassed the pain and loss she has suffered. That is why she is such an amazing being, because she chooses to feel it all. She has a good sense of what life is all about, but she was unable to let go of some things or learn how to use her struggles as strengths. She chose not to help herself. Or perhaps she didn't know how to help herself. Either way the result has been the same. Watching her suffer has been both challenging and painful.

I believed that I would never be able to pick myself up after certain heartaches and emotional setbacks. When I actually stopped to and asked myself if this was really true. The answer was of course: No.

I remember early on making it a point to always pull myself together, pick myself up and carry on no matter what had happened. It hurt my heart to see my mom that way, fragile and vulnerable. I would not become my mother—sad and broken hearted. In an effort to avoid getting hurt sometimes I avoided becoming emotionally involved. Fear became my friend. Emotional disinterest became my ally.

One positive takeaway from my parents' divorce is that it only had the power to condition me up to the point of me being aware of it. I could have gone through life fearful, doubtful, anxious and depressed, but I chose not to. I feel it in my soul that I lived this situation not to believe in defeat but to believe in the will to live and the will to love.

I now know that life is not always black and white. There is no separation between my sensitive side and my aggressive side. It is all me, all the time, rolled up into one gorgeous, complicated, perfect messy combo. To realize this was so freeing. I no longer feel stuck or pressured to "choose a side" between the extremes I have witnessed all my life. I accept that it is not that simple and that has freed me to be me.

Embracing Loss

In my life, I have experienced broken hearts both the tragedy of loss and from breakups. I have felt a million emotions under the sun, ranging from confusion, to anger, to relief.

For so long, I became buried in the dysfunction. I lost sight of who I was and what I needed. I paid more attention to what other people needed and continued to be the 'rock' everyone else leaned on. As I learned, sacrificing myself never worked for me or for the people I was trying to save. The only thing that lead to was more confusion, anxiety, and helplessness.

While these negative emotions were unpleasant, they were a necessary component to my healing.

It was these negative emotions that told me know that something was definitely amiss up and that something needed to change. When I ignored them, they continued to build internally, like an emotional cancer, but I found when I dealt with them face to face they helped pilot me to true happiness.

I am grateful to have been able to experience emotional awareness and take control in most of these situations, but there have been some circumstances that I was unable to control.

There have been two people who have held a special place in my heart who are now gone from my life—my grandmother and my best friend Matt. We all deal with experience loss. It is part of life. Without the dark there is no light. It is the contrast that makes the joyful and happy times significant.

Some people don't actually start living until they lose the ones they love. I am one of those people. It's amazing how crystal—clear the meaning of life becomes when the loss of life occurs.

My grandmother was the matriarch of our family. She lived with me most of my life and l saw her more as a mother figure than a grandmother. She took on some of the motherly duties that my mom sometimes could not bring herself to do because of her depression. My grandmother was sassy, funny, a great cook and always put her family first, especially my brother and I. This sacrifice made me feel such love. This is a huge part of who I am today. I believe that life is not worth living if you can't share it with the ones you love. No matter when my time comes to leave this earth, I am confident that the people I love will know it and that I have proved that throughout my lifetime. When she died, I was devastated. I felt as though I had lost my mother.

I also lost a piece of my heart when my best friend Matt died. I met Matt in High School and we dated for three years, until he went into the US army. I never wanted him to be put in harm's way, but I did not wish to sway him from a life-long dream. I dreaded he would end up as just another statistic.

When he was killed while deployed with American troops in Baghdad, I was crushed. I suffered from sadness, loneliness and despair.

He taught me more in those three years we were together than I could even comprehend at the time. Our commitment to being there for being there for each other no matter what gave me new perspective on supporting someone through difficult times. He broke it off with me when he was deployed. I found it impossible to accept. It took me a long time to accept his decision but I had no choice to. So much was left open and unsettled; However, I didn't let the tumultuous emotions of the break up get in the way of being there for him.

With the passage of time I continue to gain more insight from our all too short time together. He is a major reason why I became an entrepreneur. Seeing his determination to follow his dreams and the bravery required to join the army and serve his country was inspiring. Determination is an essential part of being an entrepreneur, and he was a role-model for me. Initially I was unable to reconcile with our breakup and my loss but I have now come to terms with it and have found peace with the situation.

I understand now that there are many things realize that I don't have control over and that there are also things that I may never comprehend, but I do know that in order for healing to occur, I needed to accept.

When we stop looking for all the answers, turn off our thoughts and just live as we are, the answers reveal themselves. My silver lining in the losses that I have suffered is that when I lost my grandmother and Matt, I found myself. I took the time to re-discover who I was, and re-discovered my love for life again. In the words of Abraham Lincoln, "Nothing valuable can be lost by taking time." There is a reason that "OK" is in the word broken. There will always be pain, but there will also always be strength and I know I will always be okay.

Awakening through Isolation

My most recent moment of awakening came through isolation. I left my hometown after 28 years. A year prior, I ended a seven-year relationship. I left my mom, my brother, my best friends, the only life I knew. I had no idea what I was doing with my life. I was certainly not where I wanted to be. After living on my own for the previous 10 years, I moved from Long Island, NY to Connecticut with my dad. I never dreamed I would live in CT. He was in NJ while I spent my entire life in NY.

My emotions surfaced when I finally gave myself some necessary alone time. I had emotions I didn't even know existed. You can imagine what suppressed emotion looks like after 28 years. It was terrifying and extremely uncomfortable. Despite the discomfort, I vowed to stay open. When I did, everything changed. Opportunities flowed to me naturally, people flowed to me that I was aligned with. I felt happiness in such a new and exciting way.

I realized that if I wanted to change, I had to do the work. Growth and change aren't loud. They won't make a grand entrance. You grow most when you are quiet. Change happens in moments not in a tsunami.

I have a choice every day to change my story and so do you. My happiness, my strength, my struggles and my experiences are what I have to move me forward in life. Yes, there are others there to support me, but this is my life, not theirs. I made the choice to start with myself and not to give up on myself. I learned to make myself happy and to trust that the rest will figure itself out. I have lost many versions of myself as well as those near and dear to me along the way. I understand now that no one is at fault here, and that we are all on our own path of personal growth and development.

Learning Patience

There is no timeline for growth. Having compassion for myself during vulnerable times helped me navigate the bumpy roads of change. I have noticed that I suffer most where I want the most change while failing to give myself credit for where I am today compared to where I was yesterday, a month ago or even a year ago. I now meet myself exactly where I'm at and embrace the ride. I patiently and (sometimes) uncomfortably await the adventures that I'm not yet ready for but are destined to experience.

I have learned to trust the process of personal change and growth. And I have learned to trust myself. I believe that I am always exactly where I am meant to be at any given moment in time. Everything that has happened to me up until this point has provided me with the knowledge and strength to enable me to make choices and decisions that will serve me well. This is true whether I need to let go, move on or sit with a feeling for a while. I listen to what I feel and I trust it.

There is a constant battle between light and dark within me. I have been told I am a restless spirit. I am a seeker and I love to be stretched and to continually grow. It's true that I found comfort in fear and negativity. It is familiar. All my life, I vowed to be wildly uncomfortable in this fear and negativity until I decided not to be. We all have this choice. I decided to get in the ring with my fears, my negative thoughts, and my conditioned beliefs and come out a winner. I refused to let the past write my future.

I accept that my experiences are part of who I am – but I do not let them define me.

There are many layers in life and spiritual and emotional growth demands that we peel away the layers and examine each one. As we confront our fears and deal with our pain we see that we grieve for that which has given us great joy. Pain and pleasure are inextricably intertwined.

In the end although I acknowledge the pain, I choose to remember the pleasure and revel in the beauty of my life.

My biggest lesson learned is that in order to get out, I must go in. I must heal myself from the inside out. I had to face my fears, and, well, there were a lot of fears. We aren't given anything in life that we can't handle. I believe we suffer most where we crave change the most. Sometimes, there's a bit more work to be done before we're ready to fly. I wasn't ready for a while, much longer than I was comfortable with. But my life changed when I heard the universe whisper, "She's ready."

About Lisa Laura

Lisa Laura is an Empowered Life & Leadership Coach specializing in the mind-body connection.

Lisa Laura is someone who craves depth, creativity, inspiration and passion out of every corner of life. She now brings this into her coaching practice as a Certified Health & Wellness Coach.

She believes that all that really matters in life is how we feel and if we don't feel good in our body and in our mind, what the heck is the point?

Lisa focuses on getting the mind and body back in balance from the inside out. She helps people of all ages who have lost their purpose in life and who feel stuck, find new perspective and follow their dreams again in a way that feels good to them.

Through her transformational coaching she opens doors with her clients to self-love and self-acceptance that lead to a feeling of freedom, peace and a new fulfilled life experience. She works with her clients through one on one, group and self-paced personalized coaching programs and interactive workshops. She is also set to launch creative product lines and wellness retreats sure to offer the support you need as you journey along your path. Every day she is on a mission to inspire change and offer new perspective to the ones who crave a more fulfilling life.

Her motto is "Change the way you see yourself. Change the way you see the world".

Website:	Logicallylifted.com
Email:	http://LogicallyLifted@gmail.com
Facebook:	/LogicallyLifted
Twitter:	Twitter.com/LogicallyLifted
Instagram:	Instagram.com/LogicallyLifted
Location:	Glastonbury, CT 06073

If The Dream Is Big Enough, The Facts Don't Count

by Henry Balzani

My grandparents were Italian. It goes without saying that food was an integral part of my life growing up—it was not just sustenance—it was a feast served with love. Sunday, at Grandma's house was an occasion to behold—the gathering of the clan. Food was the center of attraction not only at celebrations, but also had restorative powers. Zabaione was not a dessert—it was a tonic used by grandma when someone was weak or run down. Honey and lemon was the cough syrup of my childhood. Meals consisted of produce grown in the garden and meat from the butcher around the corner. My grade school friends teased me when I told them I had "pesto" for dinner—they didn't know what they were missing.

This story is inspired by food in all its glory and deliciousness. Food can heal the heart, the soul, and the body. Food has changed over the years, now processed, and filled with powerful additives and unknown drugs. Now my beloved food has a dual role of being harmful as well as beneficial. This is a story of how my life came full circle—from an initial passion with food, to a career in medicine and then a career in nutrition. It is a story of persistence, together with a large amount of well-timed and well-placed, people, events and a few "higher power" interventions

My parents were a wonderful combination: my mother a relentless teacher and my dad—street smart and common sense—a rare commodity these days. Together they were my guiding lights. They instilled in me a sense of love and support. They encouraged me to realize my full potential and supported me in my many ventures. Mom must have known that I had ADD, although in those days it wasn't known as that—and she maintained a quiet zone for me to use as a study. She guided me, (actually more like pressured me!), to study with regular monotony. After school I wasn't allowed out of the house to play without doing one or two spelling or math mimeos.

I did well in grammar school, but St. Peter's Prep was a different story. The Jesuits told me I asked stupid questions and despite long hours of studying, my grades were mediocre. This muted and humbled me. I began to doubt my abilities.

Around this time, I began to have an interest in pharmaceuticals.

My parents sent me to the pharmacy monthly for Modess and citrate of magnesia. The pharmacist working behind the glass partition, looked mysterious as he mixed his potions and dispensed his pills. I was intrigued.

Fordham Pharmacy School was my next step. I found the classes very interesting, and I loved being on the tennis team. I completed my first year successfully and was in my second year when my father passed away. Like it was yesterday, I remember being awakened by his fall. It was 4 a.m. I ran into the kitchen and found him on the floor. I woke up my mom, who told me to wait downstairs for the doctor. As I waited, I told God that I would be a much better person if He just let my dad live. But He had different plans. I was eighteen and I was scared. But I didn't let mom see that. I was fortunate in that my dad's death benefits covered the cost of the remaining college years. I was also lucky enough not to be drafted into the service. In some ways, luck was on my side. I had a few pre-med students in some of my science classes. They were always stressed out. They needed A's to get into Medical school. I had some vague interest in Medical school, but the expense was out of the question, and at that time the idea of becoming a doctor scared me. I was not quite ready.

I did however, have a strong interest in drugs and how they affected people. I realized that drugs were used not only for their healing qualities, but also for their mind altering qualities. Understanding addiction and substance abuse became a passion. I read every book, and every article on the subject (in those early years of drug abuse literature). I attended lecture after lecture on the topic and befriended a pharmacist with the same interest and completed my Pharmacy internship at his pharmacy. Together we lectured in schools, managed the jail pharmacy, worked with the local police and hosted a drug hot line. We handled calls from scared kids and nervous parents, counseling them and referring them for treatment when needed. Being of service to these people brought new meaning to our lives. Hearing a sense of relief in their voice meant everything. This was rewarding work on the forefront of addiction (in the 70s), but not without risk.

My first up close and personal experience with alcohol addiction, was with a neighbor, John. His wife called and asked me to come to their apartment, across the hall. He was drunk and waving his loaded 357 handgun around. I sent his wife across the hall. I spent the next two hours trying to calm him down. He was suicidal. I asked repeatedly for the gun. Finally, he gave me that gun, which I put into my back pocket (first time I handled a gun). Moments later he came out of his bedroom with a loaded 45 automatic. Great—now we both had a gun. He insisted his doctor had to take him to the hospital to be treated for his alcoholism—if not he was going to commit suicide. He had the doctor on the phone and in his anger he fired a shot into the floor. The doctor then wisely, refused to come over and called the police. When the police knocked, John sent me to answer the door and he stood at the other end of the hallway, with the gun pointed at the door, AND ME. I opened the door, the police saw the gun and jumped back. I was standing frozen, but my pants were dry. As luck would have it, one of the cops new John and said" hey John it's me Joey". Recognizing the cop, John lowered the gun, and they rushed past me handcuffed him and took him to the hospital. We were both alive, I went home. God still had plans for me. John returned after rehab and remained sober. We remained friends until he moved away. Helping people with their prescriptions and drug related questions from behind the pharmacy counter was satisfying. This encounter added a new dimension to me, increasing confidence and the ability to help people under stress.

I still thought about medical school, but I was still scared. I was not ready. I maintained a keen interest in drugs and decided to pursue a Master's Degree in Pharmacology. I understood that having an advanced degree could be helpful if I ever decided to apply to medical school. I completed a Master's Degree on marijuana. The mice were happy. I did my research during the day and worked in a pharmacy nights and weekends. After completing my Master's, I realized that lonely days in a lab doing research was not for me.

I wanted to work more closely with doctors, so I choose to work in a hospital pharmacy. I was working in the methadone clinic for a few months when the MDs running the program moved. It was at this time I was put in charge. I was interviewing patients and deciding their dosage. I was also given a beeper for hospital emergencies. This started me thinking. I had a beeper, I was interviewing patients and I was deciding their dosage. If I had a degree and a license, I would be a doctor. I was finally READY.

My goal was clear. I've heard it said "If the dream is big enough the facts don't count". I soon saw that this is so true. At this point any doubts that I would become a doctor fell on my deaf ears. I received forty (yes, 40) letters of rejection to US and Canadian medical schools. I refused to accept defeat. Each letter assured me I was a great guy, with great credentials, but my grade point average was holding me back (3.4 grade was nowhere near a 4.0). I was thanked for my interest and wished all the best in my future. It was then that I changed jobs to work in the hospital pharmacy connected the medical school. I managed to finagle an interview with the dean of admissions. He proceeded to tell me I already had a profession and would be taking a chance away from someone else. This was my 41st rejection. I was sad and depressed, but I knew I had taken this job for a reason. Something would happen. And something did happen. Some people call this luck, but I know different. I was making my own luck.

The head of anesthesia heard I was applying to medical schools and told me one of his anesthesiologists was recruiting for the Philippines. I sought him out and applied.

School was taught in English, a definite plus, some were taught in Spanish! But where the hell was the Philippines! A few months later he told me to call the dean overseas. The school was run by a husband and wife who were both MDs. The husband was giving up his position as dean for a career in politics. His wife was the chairperson for the Dept. of Pharmacology, and was now the dean. When I finally had a chance to speak with her she sounded disappointed when she heard I was twenty-eight, married, and had a six-month old daughter. When she realized I had a masters in pharmacology, her voice changed.

She asked if I knew how to use a BECKMAN SPECTROPHOTHFLUROMETER and would I be able to teach her professors to use it. It just happened to be the machine I used for my Master's Degree. Two weeks later, while I was in Mexico applying to Guadalajara Medical School (taught in Spanish) I received my letter of acceptance!

Excitement outweighed fear, pictures of poverty in the Philippines looked quaint, and I was too naive (or too stupid) to be scared. I had caught the bug and there was no cure. Come hell or high water, I was going to be a doctor. Passion has a way of diminishing barriers and obstacles. You are able to see past incredible difficulties and only see your goal. It was as if I knew this was a dress rehearsal for the stress that would come with being a doctor. This was the beginning of a stressful, exciting, and adrenaline-fueled life. All we had to do was pack up all our stuff, put it in storage, apply for loans, and move halfway around the world—I had finally realized where the Philippines was. We would be moving with our daughter—just six months old—to a country under martial law—what was that anyway? And who cares! We knew no one, and were flying into an airport that had been burned down the year before. We then had to book a hotel, find permanent housing, and register for school. Easy peasy. My only thoughts were that school was in English, not Spanish. I was the luckiest man alive! Thinking back, I realize the insanity of going to school in the Philippines. I think of the risks that we took, and a chill comes over me. But at that time it was all about the Dream.

One of the new pharmacists at the hospital was Filipino, and she asked for a picture of my family. She sent it to her family so they could meet us at the airport. I obliged, expecting nothing, and was I ever surprised. After a twenty-four-hour charter flight, we arrived at midnight, to a crowd of people waving our picture. It was amazing. They brought us to their home, gave us their daughter's bedroom, while their daughters slept on the floor. We became part of the family. They fed us, found us housing right across from school (important), and helped us with everything. This was an amazing experience and as I came to learn, very typical of FILIPINO hospitality: over the top.

My Filipino classmates were all about eighteen years old, compared to them I was a senior citizen at twenty-eight. When they found out I had a daughter, they nicknamed me "papabalzani". A few weeks after I started school, my six-month old daughter had a grand mal seizure early in the morning. Under curfew, no one was allowed in the street overnight under penalty of arrest. Scared shitless, shirtless, and in shorts, I put my finger in her mouth and ran across the street to the hospital ER. After a few days of observation, (I stared at her breathing for a full day), she was released, never to seize again. I just had a belief that everything would be all right, and it worked. We completed her work up back in the states. Her next adventure was chewing ice and swallowing a piece of the glass, while doing so. My professors assured me it would pass. There was no blood, thank God, and she was fine. Our challenges continued. My daughter and I also developed primary complex TB and we both took medicine for two years. Finally, my severe case of amoebiasis was cured with multiple courses of medications.

The first three years of Medical school, we attended classes, and we became very close to my fellow American classmates. We moved next to two American classmates and became a big extended family. We gradually grew accustomed to the heat and the major culture shock. We returned home for two months between first and second year. Fourth year was all clinical work, with as much hands on as you could handle (and I really mean hands on). We were delivering babies, assisting in operations, treating every tropical disease imaginable (including my amoebiasis), and amputating limbs. We were tasked with pronouncing infants dead, and restraining electroshock patient during treatment. In the provinces, which were outlying areas in the jungle, we would treat machete wounds packed with sugar and gasoline. I delivered babies in Neepa huts, and transported dying children to the local hospital. The conditions were brutal, unlike anything we had seen before. It was a make or break year for most students, especially Americans. The majority of the time you were on your own, making life and death decisions, and then living with the results. To survive mentally, you ignored your fear and just took care of patients. Pronouncing infants dead, was the most intimidating task. After you pronounced a child dead, mom would wrap the child and take them home to be buried (gulp). It was gut wrenching and heart breaking, as you stood in a large open air pavilion, with all the mothers staring at this foreign doctor.

We had basic medical equipment, but more importantly, we learned to develop our hands, use our eyes and all our senses to diagnose without equipment. This was a fantastic skill which is barely taught in the USA. This hands on approach, brought a closeness between you and the patient, without words. We monitored the entire labor with only our hand on the abdomen, counting the minutes between contraction, and listening to the baby's heart with a stethoscope. We were the fetal monitor machine. This literal hands on practice saved me from a false lawsuit early in my residency. Delivering an infant in a Neepa hut, with the whole family watching and the animals underneath, was only one of the highlights of my years in the Philippines.

We returned home after four years with a second child (yes, we kept our eldest daughter in spite of her antics). I then had to attend a Fifth Pathway for foreign students, so we could be reintroduced into US medicine. Although I had an MD degree, we were considered full time students and had to pay tuition for this transitional year in the hospital. I was now a full-fledged MD and again a full time student, again working nights and weekends in a pharmacy to pay for an apartment, and receiving food stamps so we could eat. Times were tough, but then so was I.

I was accepted in OB-GYN residency in my Fifth Pathway hospital. Wow, I was finally gainfully employed, if you could call it that. In those days residents' hospital hours were brutal. Today it's a different story. First year we were on call (in the hospital for twenty-four hours) every other day and every other weekend (Saturday seven AM till Monday evening when all the work was done, (SIXTY hours). For the next year we worked NINETY hours one week and ONE HUNDRED THIRTY hours the next. I calculated my hourly pay to be one dollar and change per hour. Not enough for a family of four to live on. I was forced to work my off weekends in a pharmacy all day Saturday and Sunday. Sleeping was a rare commodity. More often than not it was a cat nap trying to drown out the screams of women in labor. Eating was not a priority, it was done for survival. There were occasional meals, provided by the hospital (yuck), lots of coffee and snacks brought in by the ever generous Filipino night nurses.

Our hospital was a high risk referral center for OB, so we saw an amazing variety of patients, many of them with heart wrenching stories. We were on call so much, we practically lived with these patients through their ordeals. In my spare time—which was almost non-existent—I did have to work outside the hospital. I worked one night a week in Planned Parenthood and we covered clinic deliveries in a nearby hospital. Back in the day, (I love to use that phrase), we were supervised by attending during the day, but at night attending doctors were home. It is not like that anymore. In those days we made our own diagnosis, and had to decide if and when to wake the attending at home. God help you if you made the wrong diagnosis, or called the attending too early for a delivery. It was a crazy, but an amazing four years.

Life was about as hectic as could be, trying to stay afloat financially and staying awake. There was so much to do, and learn. We lived by the axiom "see one, do one, teach one". Beratings by the attending taught you to keep your head down and focus on the job. You subconsciously learned to subdue emotions as a means of defence and self-survival. As I write this, I am very much aware that I did a good job at that. I also learned to be stoic and always be the smiling happy face on stage as the rock for the patients.

Sometimes feelings did get the better of me. I was assigned to a fifteen-year-old about to give birth. A baby having a baby. Her parents left the hospital and told me the baby was already given up for adoption. She was so scared; she couldn't stop crying. She developed preeclampsia (high blood pressure) so I stayed with her through the night to medicate her and keep her calm. She delivered safely and a few days later as she was leaving the hospital I secretly slipped her a little teddy bear. I couldn't help myself. And I know it made a difference for her. When she matured and moved on, she became my private patient until she and her husband moved away.

After residency, I decided to open a solo practice, which required yet another loan, and the continued need for more jobs till my practice took off. I was now on call, twenty-four/seven. I went to sleep with my pants, shirt and socks next to the bed, ready for the quick trip to the hospital. Time off was non-existent. Surviving the early years of medicine was the hardest challenge of my life. Many young doctors, either cracked under the pressures, or committed suicide. I experienced this tragedy first hand when I found a young resident dead in the on call room—a needle in his arm. Long hours, little or no sleep, was only one piece of the puzzle. We made life and death decision each and every day. Each decision made, weighed heavily on our minds. We were told that each of us would be responsible for a section in the cemetery. The stress was tremendous. Then there were the mounting bills and loans from medical school. This combination took its toll on our personal lives. My wife and I grew apart—in part because I was never there—and we eventually divorced. I remarried several years later and together we ran a successful practice for many years.

OB-GYN had an 80/20 rule. Happy most of the time and sad about 20% of the time. Delivering good post-op news, to scared relatives, moved them from anxiety to happiness. Delivering babies was a mixed bag of emotions. Nine months of office visits, assuring the new mom to be, that everything is and will be fine—never really knowing how the delivery will turn out for sure. Then came the frantic call or call at three AM. After their admission to labor and delivery, its "game on", sleeping with one eye open until called upon to deliver. A successful doctor must create the ILLUSION of being less stressed than the patient, even at three AM. Events change in seconds during labor, going from serenity to sheer panic—and trying to keep this change below the patient's radar. Then comes the electric moments surrounding the delivery. Everyone is looking to see the expression on my face, as the delivery progresses: no fear, no doubt. Can't let them see you sweat. Keeping that positive expression on your face during those stressful minutes before the baby cries, can at times, be a difficult feat. Every delivery was amazing, and beautiful, but also had the potential to be a complete disaster, involving not only one but two patients—and occasionally three. I have on occasion seen a dad hit the floor! The stress of delivering a PERFECT baby, allowed for only a few seconds of joy for the delivery. The next thought was, had I done a good enough job, NOT to be sued?

My role, in the office, was part doctor, part psychologist, and part nutritionist, with not enough time to do justice to each. Young adults were always a challenge, and I found it most rewarding to guide them to the right path. To accomplish this I would give them my DAD talk. Seniors, reminded me of my mom who had passed years before. My time with them was slow and deliberate, with a little humor to reduce anxiety. On the evenings that I was fully awake, I remember going home from the office with a little smile on my face, feeling I had done a good job helping patients that day.

The universe helped me a few more times by pitting two jobs in place for me. I became Director of a Teen OB Clinic, and Director of a Substance Abuse Clinic. My substance abuse knowledge was self-taught, from books, journals, and my experience with addicts. This was the early years of drug treatment; protocols were changing with each new journal article. I was just winging it, and pretty well I must say. We were admitting about five thousand patients a year. I was updating new protocols and developed a detoxification program. Treating these patients on the forefront of addiction, seasoned and hardened my soul. After about ten years, I burned out from the daily abuse and cursing I received from the addicts, who demanded more drugs every day—I resigned.

With my newfound free time—little as it was—I now became Board Certified in OB-GYN, and added Laser Hair removal, Collagen, Botox and leg vein ablation to my practice.

During yearly years of private practice my health became problematic. I developed Atrial Fibrillation (an irregular fast heartbeat), which still plagues me. I was put on numerous medications over the years, each change requiring a weekend hospitalization for observation and cardiac monitoring. These medications slowed and regulated my heart, but unfortunately they also slowed my brain and my metabolism. After numerous, near syncopal episodes—where I almost passed out—I underwent three cardiac ablations (Strapped to a board, with a wire inserted through my groin going to my heart, they created BURN lines in my heart. Then they shock you to see if it worked, all this while only lightly sedated, ouch.) I was cured, no more medications, at least for a while. I had just celebrated my fifty eighth birthday (the age my father died), and I was getting nervous. Through all my health problems I had enjoyed training and weightlifting, when I felt good. Now I was reading everything I could about nutrition, supplementation, longevity, and age management. I went for training at Cenegenics and A4M, The American Academy of Anti-Aging Medicine. This led me to open an Age Management and weight loss practice. Nutrition became my new passion. I had to let patients know the truth about nutrition and dispel the old misconceptions (just lies). Back to my beloved Food. After years of taking a back seat to my work, food was finally back on the front burner—both literally and figuratively speaking.

I found it increasingly difficult to function well in the days following many all-night deliveries, so we closed the OB-GYN practice. We continued the Wellness practice for a few more years because I enjoyed the fact I could spend time with patients discussing health and nutrition. After a few more years, high malpractice insurance and shrinking reimbursement forced me to close the practice and retire.

I tried to keep busy during my retirement. I became a consultant for nutrition and wellness in other practices. Health hurdles kept on getting in the way, but these were only minor hurdles to jump over to be able to continue the marathon of life. Knee surgery, a hernia repair with removal of part of my intestines, were only the appetizers before the real diagnosis. I was attending an Age Management conference alone, when I received a call from my urologist telling me that the new test he performed showed I was at high risk for prostate cancer. I was standing alone, in a long empty hallway outside the conference, frozen, for a minute as I turned off my phone. In that minute my analytical brain muted the fear button and began its learned process.

Wait, my PSA tests were all normal, so why did he do this new test, was there a higher intervention? I was sure things would be fine. I underwent the biopsy, developed a severe infection, was hospitalized, and my Atrial Fibrillation returned. My biopsy came back positive for early Cancer, crap, this was a big hurdle. I was up for this hurdle, I had lots of practice. I decided on a complete removal, a Radicle Robotic Prostatectomy. Some pain, a catheter for a while (ouch). Follow up testing showed I was Cancer free, Phew, survived that hurdle. What's next? Bring it on! A hip replacement was next. I prepared well by going to physical therapy two months BEFORE the surgery, and it payed off. The surgery was at seven AM, and after three physical therapy sessions in the hospital, I WENT HOME the SAME DAY OF THE SURGERY at six PM. Recovery was slow but went well. These last couple of surgeries kept me on my ass for longer than I would have liked and reawakened my "food for enjoyment" Italian gene. Curbing this gene gets harder with age, but it is just another hurdle to overcome. Back to the gym, start from scratch again.

Life has taught me that we grow personally the same way a muscle grows. You need to be put under increasing stress to make it grow. Having undergone many stresses in my life, I had grown strong and resilient enough to grow and survive my various health problems. After all, "It is not the strongest of the species that survive, but the most adaptable. Each of these hurdles took something out of me, affecting my health. Each was a step backward in some way. But each hurdle taught me, I had to adapt to grow stronger mentally and to continue to move forward.

Instead of dwelling on my fate at age sixty eight (it rhymes), a silver linings thought came to me. Reinvent yourself Henry, and do something you love—FOOD... not eat it, but teach about food. I still had a spring in my step, and we were back exercising, and removing gluten, sweets and alcohol from our diet. My background and life's passions fit easily into the role of a health and nutrition coach. I enrolled in a Holistic Health and Nutrition Institute to continue my life's work. I have spent forty years treating OB-GYN patients and drug addicts. Now I would follow a new path to help people remove old bad habits and replace them with new sustainable healthy habits.

Most seniors would have just lived out their years quietly, babysitting and vacationing (both are my favorite pastimes). But they alone were not enough for me, I NEEDED more! I was alive again, reading, studying, and excited to help people develop their own sustainable healthy lifestyle, in this time of conflicting health and nutrition information.

Looking back, my initial focus as a child was food, then I switched my focus to PHARMacy and Medicine. My focus has gone full circle and I am now back to healthy Food and FARMacy.

My Dream was my purpose, and my Passion was the fire to keep me excited. My Preparation was begun by my parents, Persistence and Resilience developed along the way after overcoming all the roadblocks and hurdles that allowed me to grow and develop. I have told my daughters at an early age, that they could do anything they put their mind to, and all my grandkids have a paper weight that says,

DREAM BIG, WORK HARD, NEVER GIVE UP.

About Henry Balzani

Henry Balzani is a Holistic Health and Nutrition Coach, and a retired MD, with an avid love of cooking delicious Italian meals (in a paleo, gluten free way). He also enjoys reading, and weightlifting. He has experienced an eclectic life in the health field, caring for his many patients. He moved from Pharmacy, to 30+yrs of a Board Certified OB-GYN private practice, while also treating, counseling and lecturing on Drug and Alcohol Addiction.

Overcoming the many hurdles in life, to get to and through medical school and private solo practice, taught him valuable lessons to pass on to his clients. The motto "Dream Big, Work Hard, Never Give Up" has served him well to get over those hurdles.

Major health issues, including, Cardiac, Cancer, and Joint replacement that surfaced in retirement, led him to complete training at a Holistic Health and Nutrition Institute, to be able to focus on Health and Nutrition Coaching.

His purpose and passion is to help, both men and women, establish their individual, sustainable lifestyle, through real food and activity, to be able to enjoy a fulfilled life. He will guide clients with support and reinforcement during their time of transformation, and help them make their way through this era of conflicting health and nutrition information.

E-mail: http://Hnkbalzani@optonline.net
Cell: 973-997-7459
Location: Totowa, N.J.

Physical Transformation

Acknowledging the Past, Creating the Future
by Chris Holley

I discovered that I have passion for helping people achieve what they once believed to be impossible. I discovered this calling, and found this passion, through personal experience. Tired of living an unfulfilling life, I chose to redefine my life and my mindset. Since making this change I have helped many others do the same and achieve new levels of personal success – from increased self-confidence, weight loss and the completion of 5K marathons to Ironman Triathlons. My name is Chris Holley and this is my story. I'm a Certified Holistic Health Coach at Chris Holley Health & Wellness and Triathlon/Swim Coach at Evolution Multisport in San Diego, CA.

When I was 23 years old, was running my own IT consulting business. The hours were insane—sometimes 90 hours in a week! I was trapped in a perpetual cycle. Get up, go to work, go home, go to sleep—hit reset and do it all over again, day after day after day. I believed that if I succeeded in my career I would be judged as a success in life—that I would measure up. The pressure was enormous.

Today success is often measured by how much money we earn, how big our homes are and the expensive cars we drive. The perception that wealth equals success. There is a false belief, or misguided hope that as long as you work hard you will be a success.

I personally believed that men in particular had to achieve a certain level of financial success in order to be viewed as successful. The machismo effect. You know what I'm talking about—the hunter and gather: the responsibility to provide, protect, and defend. I honestly believed that having a solid career made me a better a more attractive prospect to women. I was working myself into the ground to provide for a family that I might never have. In reality I was simply working myself to death and making myself incredibly miserable in the process.

My weekends consisted of partying, sleeping and hangovers. I was spinning out of control. Drugs became part of the weekend routine. Cocaine, pot, crystal meth, and ecstasy. I was paying a hefty price for my lifestyle: $800 each and every weekend and my happiness quotient: zero. I was smashed every weekend and I didn't care about anyone or anything going on around me. I thought I was king of the world and that everyone liked me, because I was funny.

Self-medicating made me forget that I was overweight and unhappy. The truth was I didn't really like myself. My humor was self-deprecating. On the outside, I was the fat, amiable and lovable, balding white guy—you know the one. Everyone loves him. On the inside, not so much. I felt like the great pretender. I was involved in a never ending, losing battle with my ever increasing weight and I wanted everyone to believe I had the perfect life: money and success.

I wasn't blaming anyone else for my unhappiness or my weight issues. I knew I had control over both; I just chose not to do anything about it. My weight continued to mount. I stopped stepping on the scale when I hit 380lbs. My waist ballooned to 62" and people started to express concern about my health, but I paid them no mind.

I ate for convenience. When I wasn't working I spend my time online playing Final Fantasy XI. Immersing myself in work and fantasy I was essentially escaping reality. I blamed my lack of having a girlfriend on my weight and my looks. My self-esteem and self-confidence were non-existent. I didn't feel worthy of having a girlfriend. I had plenty of chances to date, but instead I spent more time convincing myself that I didn't want a girlfriend. "I work too much, or I don't want to feel tied down." The list went on and on. I began to pick up girls from the bar, not just to be with a girl, but to see if I still had game. To see if I could still bring home any girl I wanted. Looking back, I met a lot of great girls that deserved better than I gave them. Why did I behave the way I did? At the time I really believed that was what I wanted. I now realize I was trying to fill the emptiness in my life. Out of control, miserable and unhappy I began to believe that this was as good as it gets: my life as I knew it.

Although I found my work easy, the time demands created a stressful lifestyle. I worked hard and then I played hard. REALLY HARD. I believed that this had a domino effect on the rest of my life. Whatever the reason, I had lost my drive, my desire and my direction. I simply didn't care anymore. I simply gave up on my life. It's hard for me to write it now, but I had completely stopped caring about me.

The years passed, and I was still trapped in the same cycle of living to work. I no longer found solace staying home alone watching TV or playing video games. I had become more sociable being out with friends who gave me an audience, and the attention I craved. Being the center of attention had become familiar and it gave me a sense of belonging. Every weekend I would meet my friends at the same bar. I'd walk in and know about 80% of the people. It felt like home, and it felt like I belonged. I knew the bartenders by name and they knew mine.

In December of 2011 reality hit.

I was out with friends, somewhere in Pacific Beach—I didn't know exactly where or at whose home and I didn't really care. I was having a good time and that was all that mattered. I had no clue where the hell I was—so what?

I woke up in the hallway and managed to find the bathroom. I looked into the mirror, belonging to I knew not who and I didn't like what I saw looking back, "What the hell am I doing?" My life was a living hell. My days consisted of work that didn't make me happy, nights self-medicating on drugs and alcohol and weekends lost in time and space with little or no memory of the night before. I was in control of my destiny and this is where I had arrived and who I had become. Every choice, every decision I made had brought me to this point. So I looked at the man in the mirror and decided that it was time to make a change: NOW.

The next day, I started looking at other careers that didn't require working 80-90 hours a week. Less hours meant less pay and I didn't know if I would be able to support myself, but I wanted to try. I started using my 24hr Fitness membership. I'd had it 5 years and never used it. I started working out before work: I was up at 4:30AM and in the gym at 5-6AM. Getting up that early was hard—I used Facebook to hold me accountable to getting to the gym.

Most importantly, I quit drinking, cold turkey. It was hard. It was really hard. But I knew that if I stopped drinking, I wouldn't wake up at noon the following day hung over and I'd be more productive. I started going out and finding different things to do with my weekends. I began looking for things I would enjoy doing. Breaking the destructive cycle of drinking and sleeping meant I had more time for living—really LIVING. I had time to go out and do something like swim in the ocean or ride a bike along the shore. I stopped meeting my friends at the bars and in doing so, I often wondered if I was being selfish. I questioned my decision to leave them behind and put my happiness ahead of their friendship. Initially I worried that they would hate me or look down upon me for making the choice to not hang out with them. In spite of my misgivings, I stuck to my plan, and I slowly realized that it wasn't selfish of me at all. I had to take control of my life 1 step at a time. I had to take care of me. I owed it to myself.

I was still working 80+ hours a week at the same job. I still didn't really know how or where I was going. But the changes I had made began to make a difference: my world began to change. At this point many people say they pray that god has set them on the right path, or look to the universe for a sign that they are moving in the right direction. I didn't know if I was making the right choices but I knew I had to make changes in my life or I wasn't going to have a life. I am stubborn and I decided that I would never give up on myself again.

Then I had a breakthrough with my job. It was a step down in terms of where I was on the IT world but it came with one abundance resource: time. At the time I didn't know the wealth in personal free time I was about to receive, or how it would profoundly change my life. As I have said, in my 20's I completely sacrificed my own personal time to myself and others, in the quest to create a career, wrongly believing that if I had an established successful career then society at large would deem me a success. I took time for granted and didn't realize the cost of the sacrifice until my life was completely derailed. With my new lease on life and my new priorities in place I took a leap of faith and accepted a job working technical support for a big corporate software company. Suddenly, I was only working an 8-5 job

Monday through Friday. I took a big pay cut, but I got a personal time raise. It meant making some lifestyle changes: moving to a less costly apartment in a less pricey neighborhood. But when combined with the ridiculous amount of money I was no longer wasting on drugs and alcohol, the cut in pay was manageable. What I lost in income I gained in quality of life.

With this new found personal time, I started running a more. I was still over 350 lbs and could barely run 1 mile without having to walk/run it. I signed up for a 5K with a goal running at least 1 mile. Then I signed up for a half marathon and although I knew I may finish last, I knew I would finish. I finished in 3 hours and 19 minutes. I walked it, I ran it and I finished it. 13.1 miles. I cried when I finished – I couldn't believe I did it.

By 2012 my life was back on track. I realized how much more there is to life and that it is in our hands to take control of it. I still wasn't sure where I was headed, but it felt good to be out of the endless cycle of living to work. I finally felt like balance was being restored to my life little by little. I was gaining ground on the battle front with my weight loss and I no longer working 90 plus hours a week. I began going the gym and running with a friend on a regular basis. It was a great beginning to a great adventure that I looked forward to. And somewhere deep, inside it felt like I was heading in the right direction.

In 2013, I got a call from a friend I had met on New Year's Eve. She talked me into my second triathlon. I was 36 at the time. I completed my first triathlon in 2010, when I was trying to find myself. I didn't know it at the time, but that call to sign up for my second triathlon was going to change my life forever.

It was the ITU Triathlon in San Diego, and my initial reaction was that I couldn't do it. After some intense lobbying from my friend I finally agreed to sign up with her for a buddy combo that included sunglasses and a backpack. I was aware of the "Clydesdale" division for men who were 200lbs plus. My pride prevented me from joining that division, although I was indeed over 200lbs, I didn't want to get stuck with the "Fat Guy" division label. In a triathlon everyone wears what is known as a tri-kit, aka spandex. No matter how small or how big you are—it is non optional. I had a one piece tri kit that hugged every curve of my belly and my love handles. I felt ridiculous. I looked ridiculous. I was nervous, uncomfortable and intimidated. I was not a triathlete. I was a fat guy trying not to look totally stupid or make a fool out of myself and hoping not to die in the process. My entire body was encased in spandex for the all the world to see.

All I could think about was everyone looking at me (the fat guy) pretending to be a triathlete. I let all the negative self-talk affect my attitude because of my own insecurity and my own lack of self-confidence. The water was really cold that time of year and I didn't have a wetsuit. I was the last person to start the race in the last wave. The last of the last. With each stroke I said to myself, "One arm in front of the other." Surprisingly, I was the 3rd person of the wave out of the water. I jumped on the bike, and peddled by butt off, I was cold and I was tired. But most of all I was smiling. Pedalling along in my wet spandex tri kit, I felt like an elephant on a bike in a circus. I was still smiling though, and most of all I was having fun! At the start of the run, I was ashamed of my weight. I threw on a shirt to cover up the unsightly vision of my fat rolls bouncing up and down with every step and completed the 5K.

I crossed the finish line and felt this overwhelming sense of pride and self-satisfaction. Crossing the finish line, I felt like I had overcome all the negative self-talk, I felt a sense of accomplishment and an increase of self-confidence! I It was this race that defined me as a triathlete and would take me to the IRONMAN I credit my friend for pressing me into the race that changed my life.

A week later I had convinced myself that if I trained and got the right gear I could be good at this. I told myself that I could be the fastest fat guy at a triathlon, I could finish in the top 3. I realized at the time that I was making a declaration to myself that I could do something. I made it a priority for me. I joined the local triathlon club, Triathlon Club of San Diego (TCSD). Its members are some of the best people on this planet. I quickly signed up for the TriRock San Diego in September of that year.

I bought the right equipment, and I got an online training plan. I swallowed my pride and signed up in the Clydesdale division: I took first place. I had found something I could excel in and that I enjoyed. I felt a sense of belonging. Some people call it the bug, but there was just something inside of me that knew I had to be a part of this sport. In June of 2013 I signed up for my first half IRONMAN distance race consisting of a 1.2 mile swim, 56 mile bike, and a 13.1 run. Completed consecutively, this was a huge step for me. I knew I wasn't going to be fast. My goal was to finish before the cut off of 8 hours and 30 minutes.

I decided that this race would be a building race for something bigger, a full IRONMAN. I grew up watching the IRONMAN on TV and thought only professionals did it. In TCSD though I met regular people who had completed an IRONMAN. I thought to myself that if they could do it, I could do it! I signed up for IRONMAN Arizona on November 1th, 2014. That's right I was going to swim 2.4 miles, bike 112 miles, and then run 26.2 miles. When I finished in 13 hours, 54 minutes, and some seconds. I knew that I was able to achieve anything that I set my mind to.

I began to do more than just compete. I began to volunteer as an Open Water Swim Coach with their BOWS (Beginner Open Water Swim) group on Thursdays. It was through this I found my other calling. I have a knack for coaching people. As others noticed my rather obvious weight loss (at this time I was around 220 lbs), they started asking me how I lost weight and stayed healthy. I became a resource for them, a source of inspiration. With my newfound enjoyment in life and a renewed sense of purpose I realized that I needed to be properly educated so I could coach people effectively. What worked for me, wasn't necessarily going to work for others.

I enrolled in college and am currently taking nutrition classes, with a goal of getting a certificate of nutrition. I enrolled to become a Certified Holistic Health & Wellness Coach. As more and more people saw my own weight loss and health transformation, I began to help those around me with general advice. One of my co-workers that was struggling with health and weight, and by modifying her diet and increasing her activity she was able to get her Type 2 diabetes under control to the point that her doctor took her off her medication.

Another friend of mine, inspired by my journey found a passion for cycling and when combined with a healthier diet, was able to reduce her blood pressure so that her doctor took her off her high blood pressure medication and has given her a clean bill of health. She's now able to walk again without pain in her knees and through cycling and diet change she's participating in the "American Lung Association's Clean Air Challenge" in Alaska! Being a resource for her in both her diet/health choices and her cycling questions has been an amazing experience. It's hard to believe that I have been her role model for transformation and an attitude of never giving up on one's self.

My enjoyment in triathlons has also opened another career path. I started looking at becoming a swim coach and triathlon coach.

I'm now an IRONMAN Certified Coach and US Masters Swimming Masters Level I & II Coach and Adult Learn to Swim Coach. These changes didn't go unnoticed either. Being a swim coach really allows me to directly impact people's lives. When most people go on vacations there is almost always some sort of water recreation involved. For the people who don't know how to swim, they can't fully enjoy themselves. So by teaching people how to swim and not be afraid of the water, they can enjoy themselves so much more. By first getting soon-to-be-swimmers comfortable with the water at the edge of the pool, we are able to build their confidence in themselves. Then I teach the basic fundamentals of kicking, breathing, and arm stroke we slowly get them swimming to the other side of the pool. When you see the look on their face after they realize they just went farther in the water then they have in their life, it is simply priceless.

Recently I had the pleasure of teaching someone who has never swam before. I had the honor of giving this man the gift of swimming when he had a fear of water and no one in his family swam. I don't think anyone should be afraid of the water, and a defining moment during the lesson was when he swam across the pool. It was profoundly satisfying to hear him say it was one of the most enjoyable experiences of his life and that he couldn't wait to get back in the pool.

As a coach we have to believe in the people we're coaching. By me believing that he can do it, not only was I coaching him, I was also supporting his confidence. This is far greater reward than any amount of money could ever bring. Being able to bring life changing moments to others and allowing them to grow in their own lives and find their own joyful experiences.

In spite of being faced with adversity, feeling helpless and hopeless with my life spinning out of control, I found the strength within to take control of my life. I found hope and I found faith to break free from the conventions of success that today's society clings to. I moved beyond the traditional measures of success and made changes that not only changed my life, but the lives of those around me. I found my true self, a better version of myself that I didn't even know existed: Someone worth knowing, someone worth loving. That is my Silver Lining.

About Chris Holley

I used to be the stereotypical American male. At 30 years old I was tipping the scales at over 380lbs (that's when I stopped looking at the scale). My diet consisted of easy, fast, and convenient food. I worked 60+ hours week after week, and I had no energy left afterwards to be active or even run a mile. Finally, I had reached a tipping point where something had to change, there had to be more to life. I didn't want to become what so many others before me have done, and that's wake up every morning and take a cocktail of medications for health problems that could easily be changed with diet and exercise. I didn't want to have to get weight loss surgery, when I could make those simple yet hard choices without cutting into my body!

Almost 10 years later with a weight loss of 200lbs through diet and exercise, I'm no longer facing that cocktail of morning drugs just to make it through the day. I've become much more active by finding more time to do things that make me happy. These changes have lead me to complete several half marathons which have led to completing 2 full distance IRONMAN triathlons. I coach at Evolution Multisport coaching endurance athletes of all levels.

"When you change the way you look at things, the things you look at change." - Wayne W. Dyer

Website: www.chrisholleyhealthcoach.com
Email: chris.holley@chrisholleyhealthcoach.com
Facebook: www.facebook.com/chrisholleyhealthcoach
Location: San Diego, CA

Finding Your Voice Among the Voices
by Tracey Battle

I was scrolling through social media a few days ago reading some of those annoying quotes. You know the ones; 'Don't Give Up', 'Stay Strong', blah blah. Ok, I get it, but now what? I didn't give up, I stayed strong, I'm still doing all of that and I'm still going through it. What do you do when you hit, fear, anxiety, isolation, and sadness? When you feel all of those things at once, that's your breaking point. The 'I can't take this anymore' moment. What do you do then?

Where is the quote for that? When you get to that point a quote won't help. You may try to reach out for help, guidance or just an ear to listen, and that turns into a minefield. There will be so many voices telling you what you should do, where you should go, and how you should do it. So you go along to get along, the stress starts to build. And you have NO IDEA it's happening. What I have learned is that if it doesn't feel right—don't do it.

In April of 2014, I got the shock of my life when, after awakening to chest pains, I was told I was having a heart attack at that very moment by an emergency room doctor. And that they were preparing a room for me. "Huh?!"

The Doctor was probably used to saying those words. But I never thought I'd be hearing hear them. I looked at my son, and he looked at me. We could not believe what we were hearing. How could I be having a heart attack? I sent my son home, even though he wanted to stay, he had two jobs and would only be waiting.

My mind started racing. I was eating right, or so I thought. I was exercising, so could this really be stress related? You hear about stress being a killer, but it goes in one ear and out the other. Only people close to me knew about my struggles, and even they didn't know everything. They each told me to be mindful of stress, and to stop stressing. Easier said than done, though.

I just kept asking myself, "How did I get here?"

Once I was taken to my room and got settled, it sank in. Heart Attack. I resumed contemplating 'how I got here'? I took an immediate inventory, of my life, so much had gone on, I think one catalyst was the night I left for work and returned home in less than an hour.

"OMG, I'm laid off, what do I do?" I was in shock. "Mom why are you home, what happened?" my son. I told him to go upstairs, that we'd talk later. I had to get my thoughts together. I couldn't stay in shock long, had to go into survival mode. Job hunting, severance, how much savings do I have, file for unemployment. I was shocked at how few jobs there were, my severance was taxed heavily so it did not last long and unemployment was quickly running out.

When I received my first foreclosure notice, I immediately called the bank. They let me refinance based on my unemployment. It sounded weird, but I was desperate. Figured I'd file for an unemployment extension, until I found work. The very next month I was told that there was no money for extensions as all monies were going to the war in Iraq.

Back in the hospital, the cardiologist came in to check me out. Apparently the symptoms of a heart attack in women are nothing like those in men. Yes, we experience the pressure, fullness and pain in our chests. But we also get shortness of breath, nausea, vomiting, back, arm and neck pain. I had some of those symptoms about three months earlier. My then primary doctor prescribed medicine for Gerd, acid-reflux. There was confusion with my condition because I also had neck, arm and shoulder issues from a recent car accident. Which was heart related, which was accident related. At this point, our course of action was observation and tests.

Back staring out the window I continued my inventory; I looked everywhere for work, at first there was nothing. But once I did find work it was temporary and low paying. I tried to keep the pressure and stress away from my son but at times he was witness to an outburst or two.

I started working at the Post Office hoping to get hired. While there I got help from the state to pay my mortgage and condo fee. It was killing me but I made my payments every month. Because the Post Office was downsizing, getting hired was out of the question. And I couldn't get unemployment because I hadn't worked enough hours. All I knew was, I was right back where I started.

I felt like I was being punished. The job left me—I didn't leave it. I felt like I was going to explode. My entire body would get so tense, I actually would feel hot. This was not the first time I've felt this way. Over the years there had been many situations that brought me to that point. I then asked myself, "when will this end."

Luckily, I found out my former employer was looking for help in my old department. It was temporary but at this point who cares. I knew the job, the people, and it paid decent money. And there was a slight possibility I could get rehired.

Once decently employed, I made arrangements with all my debtors except one, the condo association where I lived. They came after me hard, garnished my bank account, leaving me with $20 in my pocket, and tried to have my car towed. They really tried to ruin my life. But I had to keep fighting for my son.

My son, my reason for being. When I was laid off, I felt like he was too. It may sound crazy but that's how I felt. I had to fight for his sake. When my company moved they offered help to employees who wanted to move closer. I took the deal, but in doing so I was a little further from family. I had no one to depend on and he only had me. As I went through difficulties, struggles, and finding my own solutions, I found I had cheerleaders. Always there after the struggles for the pat on the back, but had no answers for the difficulty in the beginning. That's when I missed my parents the most. They taught me so much.

I relied on what my parents taught me. Since I had a boy, and his father died when he was 9 years old, I recalled conversations I heard my dad having with my nephew. About the importance of taking responsibility for your actions, not following the crowd, being independent and a man of your word. I shared these conversations with my son. I told my son I would help him as much as I could, if I didn't have the answer, I would find someone who did.

One of the happiest days of my life was when he graduated from high school. And then when I told him he had been accepted to the college he wanted to attend. The five-hour drive to his school was actually relaxing, and when it came time to leave, of course I was apprehensive but I was also very proud.

I learned not to get too optimistic because the disappointments were so devastating. History proved to be accurate, my plate was filling up with issues and concerns; my house had been for sale, settlement of the house once it sold, looking for a new place, tensions at work, packing and moving when the time came. I also spent time looking for additional monies for my son's school tuition.

After the very hectic move, my son came home to a new apartment. His first year done, I saw growth in him, a kid to young man. The second year was becoming problematic. The school told me he would owe money, but I started looking for money too late. A very long story short, I could not help. He told me not to worry, he returned to school early where he worked off campus, went to class, studied and paid his debt of $5,000.

Before he came home for Thanksgiving break, he called to tell me he made his last payment. The day before the holiday, he received an invoice for another $5,000. I've never seen him so disappointed. So much so that he went out with friends and came home drunk. This worried me because of family issues with alcohol. He kept telling me he wasn't but he stayed in the bathroom so long I knocked. He said to come in, he was sitting on the lid. He said he wasn't drunk, "They said that's all I owed and I paid it, they don't understand, I worked so hard six days a week, still went to class, stayed up all night studying. Mom, I barely ate or slept."

To see my son like this was heart breaking. Knowing you have a debt is one thing but being told you're all paid up when you're not is another.

I did everything I could to help but I was barely making it myself, so I made calls, wrote letters to congress people, and even the White House, telling our story. The cards were stacked against us. My son came up with a plan. He had reduced the debt, so over the summer he would work to pay the rest before returning to school in the fall. What he didn't count on was fees and penalties that shot the debt back up to its original sum.

We also didn't count on me getting involved in an auto accident. And once again being laid off. His plan changed to getting three jobs, one to pay the school, one to help pay bills, and the third for miscellaneous. Unfortunately, it took time for him to find the first job. He did eventually and then the second and third. But not in enough time to return to school in the fall. At this point, spring semester was a distant thought, now reality sunk in, that his returning was not possible. He could not and has not returned to school, because of his debt, which had to be paid off first.

I was already feeling resentful, bitter, enraged, and distrustful, now add extreme guilt. I was supposed to be supporting him with his life, here he is taking care of me. I watched this young man go from job to job, changing clothes in the car, so tired he could barely stay awake. This is not what I wanted for him, this went deep, deeper than I could imagine. Here comes that tense, hot feeling. I had no income at this time and could not get any help. He stepped up, but I was torn between despair and pride. He later told me his father told him to always take care of me.

Laying in that hospital gave me pause to think. Many factors led to this heart attack, the list being too long to mention here. But these consecutive negative events caused such overwhelming feelings of inadequacy, alienation, disillusionment, and resentment that I lost myself in these feelings. I didn't want to be bothered with people. Now I knew what the problem was, but the cure was the issue. I listened to the voices, take this pill, do this, do that and you'll feel better. But I didn't feel better, I felt worse.

Once I stopped listening to others, I started to feel better. I'm realizing that I've spent most of my life living other people's idea of who I should be, not my own. Even not knowing exactly what I wanted was better than living someone else's idea. When I lost my parents, my support system, I was thrown in a dark room with many light switches looking for the right one. I've tried many but the light never came on.

I believe I've found the right switch, and the light is slowly illuminating the room. Negative thoughts, feelings and emotions have been building up for years. At some point in time all that negativity must go somewhere, for me it was a Heart Attack. The doctor prescribed many pills, but guess what, my body was not reacting well. The relief I needed was not in a pill, it's in me. The more I became accepting of me, who I am, what I wanted, the better I felt.

This is a Freeing Feeling. I listen to others now for educational purposes, but I take action based on what is best for me, if it's a mistake, it's my mistake.

Our life experiences can make or break us. When I was in my deepest despair, I was told I needed to be around people. That was not the answer for me. Becoming a Health Coach has brought me back to life. The lessons taught are so amazing because it's not just about food. It's about nourishing the mind, body and spirit. Learning how and what stress can do to the body. How what we eat plays a part in the big picture, helped me. When something exciting happens to you, you want to tell the world!! That's how I feel, being a Health Coach is my way of telling the world about something great!

We each must find what works for us, and if we are negatively judged for that, take a step back and look at who's doing the judging. Don't get fooled by perception, are they perfect? Be accepting, positive, and loving of yourself, anyone judging that probably shouldn't be in your life anyway.

About Tracey Battle

Tracey Battle is an Integrative Nutrition Health Coach and entrepreneur. She currently resides in Norristown, Pa. Before becoming a health coach Tracey suffered many life changing, emotional and physical setbacks. But while becoming a health coach she underwent a wellness transformation. Her stress and depression were replaced with hope and joy. Her love for cooking returned, and she found inner peace and happiness.

Being a heart attack survivor she understands very well what stress can do to the mind, body and spirit. She believes patience, love and support go hand & hand with good nutrition. Life should be celebrated, but much of our time is spent stressing, worrying, & doubting ourselves. This is a recipe for disease and illness, so serious changes need to be made. Tracey made the choice to make changes in her life. As she says, "Yes change is scary, but the alternative is scarier." With patience, love and support, from this health coach, you will become a healthier, happier, more peaceful person; living & loving the life you were meant to live.

Website: www.purechangeschoices.com (coming soon)
Email: purechangeschoices@gmail.com
Pinterest: https://www.pinterest.com/purechanchoi/
Location: Pennsylvania, USA

Spiritual Growth

A Journey From Tampons to Tombstones

by Kathy Kastner

"You can help us, I'm sure. You'll know someone in production". So said the pre-natal instructor (PNI), who – I thought – should have been directing her attention to our own 'production-in-progress' evidenced by my burgeoning belly.

The six couples in the pre-natal class had introduced themselves, and at the time I was an on-camera entertainment reporter – working in the television production business.

"You need help with…?" I grudgingly asked. "Producing videos for you expectant parents who concentrate wholly on labour and delivery with not a moment spent on the result: the baby."

I sighed. My husband – father of the baby-to-be – sighed. We'd had a super quick courtship and pregnancy came shortly before we got married, bought a fixer-upper and started new jobs. We were both in 'production': he, an audio specialist, me the reporter who could only be seen from the waist up.

We had our hands full, but –not wanting to risk putting off our teacher our guide, the woman who would teach us how to breathe through labour pains – we heard her out.

Back at home something clicked: never mind 'finding someone in production' to help: we'd take it on – with a twist: instead of healthcare professionals pontificating (with all due respect to healthcare professionals) we'd bring the 'everyman's point of view.

We'd be entrepreneurs and we'd get rich fast because there were hundreds of thousands of couples just like us – going through pre-natal classes, focused on the hours of horror that awaited us in about, without a thought of the days, weeks, months, years of horror after the baby was born.

We knew none of this at the time, but bounced back to our PNI with the great news: she'd found her team.

The 'everyman's point of view was not new to me – I'd made my name in tv as a fearless woman who put herself into every situation. I was 'bounced' from a nightclub when I did a story on bouncers; tried and failed at origami when reporting on a new DIY sensation, put on a costume for a Halloween story.

I was ready to immerse myself in the world of newborns and to work with my brand-new husband.

We tested the idea out on various friends and family. A goldmine, said they. You could get baby tapes into every hospital across the universe. The healthcare system will thank you. You'll be Mrs Mom, with Mr Mom as your side-kick.

There were those that cautioned us not to share our brilliant idea, lest it be stolen, so we got a move on. And so began our lives as entrepreneurs.

We figured there were three parallel tracks to pursue:
- Creating content
- Creating funding
- Create marketing strategy

I had no idea that my pre-tv experience – as an advertising copywriter – would play its part conquering new territory: short, snappy phrases work as well in marketing a new business as a new product. My advertising work included a Christmas ad for whiskey: "Give Generously" was on billboards across Toronto for the holiday season.

But my fave related specifically to being a woman – hence the 'tampon' reference in my journey: Midol was a product supposedly designed just for us women at 'that time of the month'. What fun, playing with words:

"As a woman you know the difference between Period pain and pain, period." Won me a couple of awards.

And so with my patchwork of experience, I felt uniquely qualified to write about anything concerning childbirth and beyond.

Back to the present: our PNI, overjoyed at her easy 'A', suggested topics that she knew freaked out new mothers: Bathing, Skincare and Vaccines.

"Let's start with newborn bath," said PNI." You get the cameraman, and I'll meet you in the hospital lobby."

Blithely, we did her bidding. We did not make it past the lobby. Hospitals, it turns out, are magnets for producers. Think of it: drama, human interest, science, triumphs and tragedy. That's even without the scripted stuff: ER, Scrubs, House. Turns out stepping foot into a hospital with a camera that's more than a smart phone requires more security clearance than bringing in firearms. We were escorted out with a bill for shooting something we hadn't even had a chance to shoot.

Before the baby bathing fiasco, I'd also gone down the funding route. Being on-camera at a major tv station gave me the cred to pick up the phone and ask to speak directly to the product manager for Pampers. He was immediately intrigued and asked me the first of many questions that became the foundation for my Entrepreneur 101 through Grad School: 'how many people will you reach with your pre-natal video'. Gah! Numbers. Not my strong suit. But I was nonetheless able to unwittingly get his help by walking him through the steps. "6 couples per 6-week class, new classes start every other week." This satisfied him enough to ask the next question for which I was grossly unprepared: "How much are you asking?" I came up with the most extravagant figure I could get past my quivering lips. He agreed immediately.

That one call gave me invaluable info: I started out too low.

So it was with the confidence of having what turned out to be a paltry amount of starter funds that I called the cameraman and marched triumphantly into the hospital lobby. Only to be marched out.

Next hospital trip – to a different hospital – I made sure ducks were in order which included negotiating with the public affairs department. This was more in the order of – again – having to think on my feet and sound the essence of in control. I thanked my lucky stars for the live tv experience which had schooled me in 'thinking on my feet'. The hospital wanted to know what they'd get in return for access to their mothers, babies, 'bathing' room, nurse-educator. "Well," I began, "our policy (Policy? My inner voice was incredulous. What policy?) is to give credit PBS-style: your logo and 'thanks' worded by the hospital" "Will we get a copy of the tape, free of charge?" (My inner voice: omg that's it? Well like yes. No brainer.) What came out was "Of course I'll make sure you get a copy."

Fast forward: within a year, we had produced videos on the three topics. They were about 5 minutes each – the length of time our PNI had advised us would be appropriate for in-class use, with time for discussion.

Now all we needed was to get them into pre-natal classes. And so my education began on the fine and not so fine points of marketing and distribution. Did I mention that my own schooling stopped midway first year University?

I'd been so certain that it'd be a 'build it an they will come' that I hadn't understood that the hard work was only just beginning.

I was fortunate to get an article in the largest national paper, which gave a lame start to marketing and distribution – via a couple of calls from hospitals.

Next, I spent months driving tapes to health departments, hoping that mass orders would result. Nada. Not a one. Then another stroke of omg: a parenting magazine called to review the tape, entitled Mom's the Word, and I realized: reviews by influencers would, could accomplish what no amount of advertising dollars could.

We began selling tapes out of our front hall. This, with a new baby, new jobs, renovating a house. Where were the millions of dollars? Where was retirement at age 30? Where was sleep? That took many more years and tears.

The next challenge was one I had not anticipated. A wardrobe challenge. I'd been voted the most popular entertainment reporter at the time, and that vote came, in part, from my ab fab out on the town duds.

I had one semi-respectable outfit to wear to a funding meeting but if there were two with the same person, the game was up.

I had to transform. And transform I did, albeit not with any great enthusiasm. But worth it? Hell yes. I could see I was taken more seriously. I walked differently. In due course, I was as comfortable in the boardroom as I'd been in front of the camera. Neither came naturally, but both were necessary.

Our Mom's the Word 'baby tape' business evolved into a whole television network – The Parent Channel - broadcasting in hospitals across Canada, That success birthed **Healthtv**, broadcasting in hospitals all across North America. At every new stage, I had to re-group, learn anew and react to the unexpected. But that comes with being a ground-breaker.

However, while congratulating ourselves on these business successes, at home it was different situation. When our second daughter was born, 3 years after our first, we were both 'downsized'. As the face of the company, I became the breadwinner and it shifted the delicate Man and Woman balance. I had to relinquish control of things I felt I was most certainly better at, but were not worth pushing for. We also had radically different working styles, expectations and standards of 'excellence'.

Yelling matches became the norm.

I worried at the impact on our daughters and so made it my mission to keep things calm when they were in the house. I made a conscious decision to be disciplined about mindfulness practice, doing yoga and getting good energy from sources other than my marriage. I think I'm as proud of my own development as a person as I am of our business accomplishments.

Eventually we solved the home-front wars situation by hub taking office space, moving the business out of living space. And eventually, an investor invested, and for the first time, we had a Financial Officer. He turned out to be a murderer. (But that is a whole different story).

Today, I continue to break ground, focusing on a topic closer to our 'murderer' than newborns: BestEndings.com - my 'laymen's point of view on having the best possible end of life and my book, Death Kills and other things I've learned on the internet.

About Kathy Kastner

Kathy Kastner is a serial entrepreneur, with a talent for layering past skills onto new concepts. From advertising copywriting and on-camera reporting to developing novel business models and embracing social media platforms she is motivated by curiosity and the joy of identifying gaps in communication. With end of life the most recent identified gap, Kathy developed the first website from a 'layman's point of view' addressing nuances of decision-making as life winds down.

BestEndings.com is utilized by health care professionals, patients and care-givers to help navigate these emotional and complex issues.

Kathy is a participant on invitation-only round-tables, think-tanks, advisory boards and steering committees and is a frequent speaker at healthcare conferences. A keen sense of humor helps her keep even the most difficult topics in a positive light, as with her book Death Kills...and other things I've learned on the internet.

Website: www.BestEndings.com
Email: kathyk@bestendings.com
Facebook: https://www.facebook.com/kathy.kastner
Twitter: @kathykastner
LinkedIn: https://www.linkedin.com/in/kathykastner
Location: Toronto, Canada

Guidance From My Guardian Angel
by Debbie Horovitch

I couldn't even open my eyes to see him throwing books around my apartment. My head and heart hurt like a piano had been dropped on me that night. Hiding under the covers, I was sobbing uncontrollably, in a fetal position, alone in bed at 4:30am.

What sounded like underground explosions sent tremors through my body, and the universe outside screamed crashing sheets of snow and water against the walls of my bedroom, over and over again, like it was trying to split itself in two.

"You're not listening!" he shouted, not in a violent or oppressive way; he was really just trying to get me to pay attention to his message. I was trying to listen, but in that moment all I could hear was the rushing sound of blood in my ears; my heart was racing as I tried to catch my breath through my sobbing.

When I got up the next morning, everything outside was covered in shimmering shards of ice, the air humming in an unusual muted silence for my midtown neighborhood. There was an eerie chill to the air inside my apartment.

He had certainly sent a message... and caught my attention—the chill indoors and destruction outside paralleled one another with eerie significance. Things had changed irrevocably and forever.

As I was taking stock of my experience from the night before and reconnecting myself to the world, I suddenly realized the power was out. We rely on energy and electricity every day. We take it for granted. I could feel a rising awareness of how fragile and equally powerful everything in the universe is.

It was the same for me as before: too much in my head, I was doing my best to work through my grief and pain alone, not wanting to burden anyone with what I thought were my secret thoughts, and convinced that my reputation was still on an upswing, even though for months I'd been screwing up one opportunity after another.

Despite appearances, I wasn't really connecting with anyone or fully embracing my own potential in life—this time my confidence had hit the breaking point and the evidence was all around me.

The tree outside my apartment window that had framed my life achievements more fully each year for a decade was suddenly split, folded over in a dramatic end-of-performance bow, bent over from wind and the weight of ice that covered every inch, forming a cage of twigs and icicle bars, encircling the base of the trunk.

From my temporary rest point in a high perch, nestled into the cradle of the tree that was perilously growing from the sheer vertical rock wall of my life, I was suddenly in freefall. It felt like I was gasping for air, struggling to breathe against the velocity of change, grasping desperately for anything at all to hold on to.

My guardian angel was telling me exactly what to do, what I had to do, and what to hold onto.

I had to find a way to empower people. I believed I was charged with helping people discover their deep well of potential in life, tapping into the confidence and curiosity that comes along with unapologetically and persistently allocating energy to exploring ALL their gifts. I didn't understand what he meant, but the message was that I had to use my tools to become all I was meant to be—by throwing books around my apartment, in my perceived reality in the moment—I was being told to empower and encourage people involved in fundraising for his favourite charity, and through that to fulfill my vision of becoming a media mogul.

But to do so, I would have to find a way to fix, motivate, and support myself first.

I was being directed to walk in my purpose, to really embrace it, to really become me. After years of knowing where to turn for quiet guidance and as needed support, I thought I would suddenly have to fight all alone.

But of everything that existed in that moment in the universe, all I could see was inside this deep well of pain and depression. The pain of loss. All I could see, hear and feel was the sense of loss and emptiness. The strongest and closest connection to my family life and my childhood was suddenly, permanently, and with almost no opportunity to say goodbye, was simply gone.

That was December 21, 2013 and my cousin Steve had passed away suddenly just a few days after my 40th birthday, four months earlier.

Two Years of Isolation That Looked Marvellous from the Outside

When I look back now, I can see the fight I was waging was against change in my life, my career, and my awareness. I was entering the last leg of the race, the hardest part—like slowly sinking to touch rock bottom, before regaining balance and buoyancy.

I thought I'd been through the worst of the most difficult personal transformation I could possibly experience already in my late thirties. But Steve's death was sudden. A shock to everyone. I was completely unprepared for how it would impact my sense of self knowledge and worth, all my connections to family and my ambition. I had lost the person in my life who had been there through it all, more than anyone else, to be a witness to my entire life.

While I was grateful to be there at the end of his life, it felt like we as a family were at the center of a spinning vortex, the calm, quiet eye of a hurricane.

As I walked away from the hospital the morning of his passing, I found myself pulled back into the sheer velocity of my life, and I welcomed the busy-ness to keep depression and my feelings of shock and sadness away.

I found myself asking "What would Steve tell me to do in this situation?" frequently in the weeks and months after he died, and most of the time his response was clear—"Do what you need to do to succeed, Debbie". It was almost like I was testing that he was actually still here. I found myself evaluating opportunities by a measurement of would Steve approve, and would he be proud if his kids took the same actions – despite losing him, could we use the sadness and negative energy to create a positive living legacy?

I had to make one of these choices immediately, the day after his passing. I decided to move forward with a livestream interview on YouTube I had planned with representatives from Kindle Direct Publishing. The livestream was a milestone conversation I'd been anticipating for almost a year at the time, since launching my show and successfully inviting bestselling book authors was probably the most assertive move I'd made for myself in years. Also, because this was an interview coordinated months earlier by a frequent guest and my primary mentor at the time, Michael Procopio, I had all the more reason to proceed. I did move forward, but still handed over much of the responsibility for live conversation moderation, to Michael.

My original intention was to time the production of this episode of #SparkleSOS Book Authors & Publishers with the launch of my entrepreneurial book publishing business, but when too many things were going on at once, I decided to put this second new business on the back-burner.

Additionally, a few days before Steve passed, I had booked flights to fly across the continent to meet and work with a long-time mentor, Mike Michalowicz, to participate in the recording of the CreativeLive.com course for his book, The Pumpkin Plan. It was an opportunity to finally meet him in person and to be part of an important experience in his business. I'd made my application to CreativeLive earlier in the summer, and heard just the week before booking my flights, that I was selected to be in the live studio audience with Mike and to potentially be documented in the recorded content of his CreativeLive course.

It was important for me to be there to participate, because Mike's mentoring and his book The Pumpkin Plan, had inspired me to create my first Google+ Hangouts on Air show, #SparkleSOS Book Authors & Publishers; a monthly mastermind meeting of book authors.

Launching my show in the twelve months before losing Steve has since proven itself to be the best quality "insurance plan" I could create out for myself. Not only was I generating awareness for myself in professional circles, I was creating new relationships and finding new influences to supplement Steve's continuing guidance.

Within a few weeks of starting to proclaim myself as the creator of Celebrity Hangouts on Air, I was beginning to realize the incredible universal value in creating something brand new in this world yourself, and driving it successfully into the marketplace.

This trip to San Francisco in September 2013 ended up being an incredibly important and engaging experience for me—I had the opportunity to spend a week in San Francisco visiting with Steve's younger brother and his family, meeting clients, prospects and guests from my shows in person, and finally connecting with Mike Michalowicz in person at CreativeLive. It was the day of Mike's birthday, on the second morning of two days of in-studio work, and we were all in such an emotionally open state that during one of our interactions while recording, contributed to inspiring Mike's third book, Profit First.

Almost all my early show guests since the launch became my friends, including many of the bestselling book authors who are my "celebrity" guests. But a year into the production, by the time I was in San Francisco I still didn't know how to monetize my shows and audiences. There wasn't really anything I had for sale, other than my available consulting services.

I've known Mike since the early days of Facebook and there were times when I had the same feeling of brotherly protection and encouragement from Mike, that I had always known I could rely on from Steve. It was weird, but I had a sense that Steve had supported me to take that trip after his death, to reconnect with my family and friends.

When we talked in between recording takes Mike encouraged and welcomed my ambitious book plans, offering to connect me with some of his contacts, and taking a position of a business financial coach (it reminded me of how Steve adopted me as his financial planning client), by demonstrating to me his Profit First Accounting method for small business that could help me manage my hot mess of business accounting methods.

The next month after returning home, I took on a new agency client in social media community management, who I lost a few weeks later, realizing they weren't a fit for my new focus in business: leveraging my new brand Celebrity Hangouts on Air and getting it out there in the industry. It was time for me to finally start focusing on myself and my own business brand successes, and start taking clear steps towards fulfilling the life direction and advice Steve had given to me.

After losing the client, and considering my options for business development I thought it must mean (guidance from Steve?) that now was the time to move forward with my own brand and business fully and honestly for the first time, by launching the first version of my online training course, Celebrity Hangouts on Air.

During that same time, a long-time friend and colleague hired me to manage the media investments and promotion of his online car sales start-up. This was a dream consulting gig for me—working with my ideal client colleague, who was my 17-year career mentor, friend, and often one of my client avatars over the years. The caveat was that they were still a pre-launch start-up so while funds were limited at the beginning, there was great potential they could quickly become a client who could sustain me on a monthly basis, allowing me the time and freedom to continue supporting the promotion of my training program, and begin writing my book of the same topic.

Not only that, they loved the approach I offered with Celebrity Hangouts on Air and started our engagement with a new car sales livestream talk show. Unfortunately, just as they launched the website, their funding was pulled and everything instantly stopped. I was paid fully for my work, but in a few hours, I had gone from planning and working on their launch for the next year, to contemplating my new business game plan for 2014.

Dorie Clark was researching and writing her second book STAND OUT: How to Find Your Breakthrough Idea and Build a Following Around It in the fall of 2013. Dorie had been a featured guest on my show after publishing her first book (Reinventing You) earlier in the year. At the time, I introduced her to the Hangouts experience and my other bestselling book author guests, including Chris Guillebeau and of course Mike Michalowicz. Following this, she asked if she could interview me for her next book, and of course I happily obliged. I felt like contributing to books created by leading business mentors would help me establish my own brand, awareness, and authority and help in the future when I wanted to approach traditional publishers about my own book.

I was doing everything I possibly could to keep myself busy, distracted, isolated, and in my emotional comfort zone. My activities throughout the speeding Fall months even included launching a new weekly livestream show as an industry example of what could be done, by anyone.

Weeks earlier, my first afternoon in San Francisco was quiet, since I didn't have roaming data on my phone yet, so I was sitting at "home" in the living room of Steve's younger brother and I was coordinating meetings with friends and colleagues for my week in town.

While watching TV that day (I was watching Long Island Medium for the first time ever, I kid you not), I was inspired by my angels to create a second-screen experience for one of my favorite binge-watching shows, SCANDAL. I had just been introduced to the show (and watched two complete seasons), in the weeks between Steve's cancer diagnosis and his passing from pneumonia. I decided to launch it as an after show for this popular prime time TV show, where we would discuss with enthusiastic guest panelists and show superfans, the episode and storylines in a format titled #SCANDALspin.

Through the four weekly trial episodes produced in October and November, we were able to demonstrate the personal human connections anyone can create, by using Google+ Hangouts on Air to create a community experience like a dinner party table, front porch, or front stoop gathering place.

I learned the incredible amount of planning work and details that could be prioritized for a Hangout production event, and realized that how well that investment is managed is directly related to the value of the outcome. It allowed me to understand the opportunity and marketplace that exists for large-scale Hangout on Air production events, like planning to tape a client's television commercial with a live-streaming audience. It lead me to see how my brand could scale its impact and manifest opportunities to help the charity organization that was in my message to support.

By early 2014 I was fully engaged in launching my business as best I could and trying to develop publicity, with a zero operating budget and no clients at all on my roster.

I kept being reminded of that stunning night just weeks earlier when Steve had made his presence known definitely, and saw my actions in business as a dedication to the guidance he'd been giving me: to follow my purpose of connecting people and organizations through storytelling events (he was throwing books around my apartment...).

With every new achievement or opportunity that came to me without effort, it seemed that I was on track to become a successful consultant for agency brands and clients' Hangouts on Air. Maybe it was a lack of self-confidence or maybe it was simply my grieving process, but I still wasn't approaching anyone or putting myself out there with offers; I wasn't actively learning about sales in my business and establishing momentum or badly needed revenue.

Lucky for me, my activities established my reputation as a thought leader in Canada about G+ Hangouts on Air productions. This, combined with my career connections and list of past agency clients and brand associations, began to attract potential business opportunities and clients. I found myself swirling trying to serve them all, or even just to get one to hire me at a sustainable level.

My first international speaking engagement for Celebrity Hangouts on Air was in spring 2014 in Las Vegas for the Catersource and Event Solutions conference for meeting planners and event professionals. This was a big step up for me since it wasn't a social media focused event, and it wasn't local. This represented a huge leap forward for me, and since I had limited international speaking experience at the time, I was happy to negotiate compensation for my flights and accommodations.

Before, I had been targeting the wrong people with a combination of the right services but wrong offers. I was offering anything and everything I could think of to help empower clients, to enable them to see their limitless power and creative potential in their lives, but nobody really understood what that could look like.

I thought I was doing what I needed to do, to follow Steve's advice to grow into my own potential for myself, but most days I was not. I didn't know that grieving is a process that takes a hold on your life whether you want it to or not—even though I felt like I was "working", I was more of a zombie than a human, and my business bottom line reflected that truth.

As best as I could I leveraged all the relationships my Hangout productions helped me create. By the summer I'd created the opportunity to *coauthor* an article for Forbes.com with Dorie Clark entitled "The Ultimate Guide to Hosting Google+ Hangouts on Air". I was surprised that I could get published in such a highly respected title my first try at submitting an article, but it was well planned and I had written it with focused determination that Forbes audience would read it. That article was highly successful in generating new positive business connections and opportunities.

To my complete surprise, the primary group of known Google+ consultants were offended by my efforts and my apparent snub to their earned position in the industry, and they responded with bullying and trolling on my social media accounts. After the initial shock of their taunts and insults wore off, I set to work responding to the few relevant criticisms and did my best to ignore the haters. My non-engagement of the angry mob publicly in social media gave me the opportunity to demonstrate to potential clients my grace under pressure and as a result, a number of people reached out to offer their congratulations and potential new business opportunities.

The Birth of The Silver Linings Storybook and Understanding My Guidance

By summer 2014, I'd had enough of the rut. I had been chasing one client opportunity after another for nearly a year, with very little results.

I needed one last isolation period but this time with a purpose. As I was experiencing the Forbes.com article wave of interest, and public response to my being bullied around my Forbes livestream production, I entered a business development program run by the City of Toronto. I'd be networking with entrepreneurs and working on completing a first business plan in almost 5 years, for my agency Social Sparkle & Shine. It was a three month program that had us "launching" our new businesses before the New Year, and I was able to use it successfully to stay focused on one project for nearly the whole fall.

I launched my new business plans with ambitious predicted revenue numbers, noting that I was planning to have single months with revenue over and above my annual starting salary. My peers were impressed, but I still felt scared and the program coordinators were hesitant to congratulate me on a "pre-launch" business plan that showed very optimistic growth.

But I was confident in my actions—Steve's spirit was showing up whenever I asked for him, and offering guidance in his twisted way that always told me it was really him.

By January 2015, I'd decided to go on a work contract for a Google and YouTube pay-per-click firm, knowing that since I'd had a similar job a decade earlier, the activity would create momentum for my own business sales and allow me to launch with a roster of fresh business-owner contacts and connections. It was a bit of a slog, but it built my momentum.

Dorie Clark's book, "Stand Out: How to Find Your Breakthrough Idea and Build a Following Around It", was finally released in May and I was thrilled to receive copies of the book from the publisher and participate in social media celebrations and chats, as her book was very well received.

Much like Mike Michalowicz's book, "The Pumpkin Plan" had inspired ideas and influenced my business activities three years earlier, Dorie's book sharing stories and experiences of entrepreneurs just like me (and including me!), also made me think about the legacy my business and life could leave. A small first step I took was to plan a new local meetup.com group for business networking and success called Social Goodwill for Business (#SoGood4Biz).

In early October, I received a brief note from Dorie explaining that she'd be in Toronto as a stop on her book / speaking tour and she was hoping to meet. After meeting her and some friends for dinner the day before her presentation, we were invited to also attend her presentation as her guests. It was a thrilling experience to sit in the large presentation hall, seeing Dorie in real life, in the room with me (after so many video, livestream, email, and social media interactions), and to hear her talking about the insights she had gleaned from interviewing her subjects, the "stars" of her book—which included me!

During her presentation Dorie spoke about when something happens to a person that suddenly creates open space in their life and mindset, this is when a breakthrough idea can come to you. She explained the logic that we all experience: when you suffer a sudden shift of schedule—from a job loss, or closing a business, a relationship ending, or any major transition in your life, from focused and challenged to lost and struggling—that is the situation when you're most likely to be struck by life-changing ideas, because your mindset suddenly has available mental energy and is searching for answers.

Did she say it could happen after a death?

Or did she talk about the classic term silver linings?

For the next few weeks I was floating through the streets of Toronto, high on inspiration combined from my ideas and momentum inspired and aided by friends, and new community in my coworking space.

I found myself consciously thinking about silver linings and started to search my own history for silver linings stories in my own life experience. I had a lot of failure and disappointment, so it seemed like there would be a lot of opportunities for me to explore and examine where I could prove the existence of "silver linings" to every "stormy experience".

But it was becoming more obvious by the day, I needed to refocus my business and start making more direct offers, unapologetically going after what I really wanted.

The more I thought about it, the more I knew that I had to bring back my publishing company idea and generally needed to stop listening to the people who were uncomfortable with my creative, sometimes twisted, perception of the world and ways of expressing myself. I needed to tell my silver linings stories, and just like how I was pulled into publishing by my peers and colleagues after so many Hangouts with book authors since 2012, I needed to change my thinking patterns and the tone of the stories I tell about myself, so that **by habit** I could learn to realize the benefits in the most challenging days.

What I've realized about my silver lining story is this:

When it felt like I'd lost the one person who loved and protected me through my life, everything came together to show me how many more positive and supportive people I have who are living, and also to confirm the reality of guiding spirits and energies.

- Steve is still here to support me, and I think he's probably more powerful now. Prior to these experiences I barely knew how much departed family are always there to support us, and how much of our actions today will create a lasting legacy for the people we love.

Even though I didn't accomplish anything directly impactful for the bottom line of my business for almost two years, I can see that my activities during those times have allowed me to emerge now stronger than ever—that it is in the triumph over dark days that we get stronger. It's impossible not to.

- There is an opportunity for deep creative richness that exists, even in the loneliness and isolation of a grieving period; as observed by Dorie Clark in her book Stand Out.

I learned the proof of the saying "It's not what you know, it's who you know, that matters most in life." and that my lifelong dreams of becoming a book publisher and media mogul are within my abilities to achieve, despite my history of experiences that others label as failure.

- Announcing that I was the author of an upcoming book and hanging out with successful book authors, in advance of the unexpected personal challenges I would have to overcome, was what gave me all the business opportunities that came to me during that period of retraction and repair.

I learned that silver linings exist in every challenging experience. In the hardest and most challenging times of our lives, are there to show us proof of how strong and capable we are of overcoming those situations. And how deserving we are of the rewards that lie on the other side of challenges.

"Life is suffering" is a statement I never fully embraced until now; I can see that it is the challenging times that delivers you to the doorstep of greatness, the opportunities to shine where all anyone else can see is repeated failure and darkness.

Look for your silver linings story in life and keep in mind that challenges are actually opportunities for you to emerge victorious where everyone else would fade away, give up, or shy away from challenges—it is your opportunity to break through to the next level!

About Debbie Horovitch

Debbie Horovitch is a media business consultant with more than 20 years' experience working with owners of businesses large and small, established or start-up, helping them leverage the most compelling and cost-efficient media channel opportunities available at the time. When she first started as a Toronto ad agency media buyer, fax and typewriters were used for every agreement!

From playing "the commercial game" while watching TV on one of 3 channels as a child in the '70s, to negotiating multi-million-dollar media campaign agreements, to becoming an independent media consultant specializing in underutilized digital media approaches—Debbie has an understanding of the media landscape that is rich and unique, and comes from her never ending fascination with the complex and changing priorities of media business owners.

Whether it's understanding where your ideal client prospects can be found, or seeing a blue ocean strategy for strategic content creation to appeal your ideal publicity in existing media channels, Debbie can help get your message in front of the right audience!

Debbie is a storytelling professional speaker who engages audiences with personal stories of challenge and struggle, looking for the humour and silver lining outcomes of challenging growth experiences.

Facebook: https://www.facebook.com/debbie.horovitch
Twitter: https://twitter.com/Debbie_h2o
LinkedIn: https://www.linkedin.com/in/debbieh2o
Website: http://theSparkleAgency.com

Author Recommended Resources

Would You... Like to Coauthor a Book With Us?

Chances are excellent you have already had a number of a-ha moments or compassion-rising experiences as a direct result of a story you read in Silver Linings Storybook: Successful Leaders Share Inspiring Stories of Overcoming Stormy Days in Personal and Professional Life.

Question: What happened? Did you suddenly recognize in your own past an experience of ongoing or acute struggle, that re-ignited your desire to pursue a childhood dream? Were you able to develop deeper understanding and empathy for someone who you previously thought wronged you in business or relationships? Are you inspired to help change the world around you, and everyone beyond, by sharing your silver linings story?

Did it involve the "sale" of anything or was it a family or social event that changed your confidence and view of the world forever? Were you able to let go of vigilance and victimhood, only to discover more of the best you've always meant to be? Maybe you took an idea or technique from Silver Linings Storybook and persuaded a son or daughter to finish school, give up drugs, or make better grades?

Whatever the circumstances, if Silver Linings Storybook played a part I'd like to know about it, and so would our readers. Your contribution can be extremely helpful and it might make the difference in the lives of everyone you meet, and many more who you never will. Tell us, in your own words, exactly what happened and my team and I will rewrite the message to reflect your own personality while adding my personal touch so that it fits the message and format of the book. Final approval will be yours.

Here's why I hope you'll respond: First and most important is the satisfaction you will gain from helping others. Second, the career enhancement which comes with the publicity for helping to write a bestseller (since you are coauthoring the book, you know it will be a bestseller don't you?), could be substantial. Third, you will have the opportunity to receive a beautiful, autographed, hard-cover version of "our" book with your name engraved in **silver** on the cover.

Respond with your story to: Debbie.Horovitch@gmail.com

What's Your Silver Linings Story?

I believe silver linings stories are happening around all of us every day, and we can see them occurring for us, if we choose to look at ourselves and acknowledge the strength and potential we possess, as demonstrated by our perseverance to get through the hard times.

We've all experienced difficult times in life—a challenging personal relationship or the loss of a loved one can impact your business and career prospects, by dampening your self-confidence. Often the easiest response to a disappointment is to deny it, to ignore it, to forget it ever happened, and simply move forward.

If you shield yourself from looking at the most painful or humiliating moments that you've experienced, it's also nearly impossible for you to recognize how strong and talented you are to have found a way through them—or a way back from them.

It's the alternate skills developed, and natural talents uncovered in response to pressure, that are your "silver linings" to your cautionary tale, or the moral of the story, that you tell with intrigue, surprise, or even highlighting the ironic humor in so many of our private moments.

Your "Hero's Journey" story is one of the most compelling types of stories you can craft and share about yourself. The ability to instantly connect on an emotional level with everyone you meet, is a powerful skill to leverage, as you're growing into the confident and compassionate person you have always desired to be.

A few tips include: aim never to harm or humiliate anyone else in the telling of your story—try to focus on what you learned, how you changed, and why it's so much better for you now that you recognize "the message in the mess". Even if you change their names or anonymize your story, they're likely to hear about how you portrayed them in your story, and it *will* impact your relationship. You have a lot of ownership in how people respond to your story—based how you engage them in the process.

It's OK to spend some time (especially at the start), writing painful stories and almost dwelling in your pain, because it gives you a rich resource of experience and memories written to craft the powerful story you *will* tell. Also, it can be very healing as most of us default to ignoring and burying our most painful experiences.

But don't dwell too long, and be sure to focus the majority of your time and focus on the silver lining that you realized *as a result of your struggle*.

As you get into the habit of looking for the silver linings in every painful past experience, you'll begin to enjoy looking at your unique & unfortunate life experiences as your own VIP ticket to gain entry to the next level of significance and impact.

Here are a few questions to help you start crafting your unique silver linings story:

1. In what ways did you have to work hard or struggle, in order to accomplish the greatest achievements in your life?
2. Are you burdened by a physical disadvantage, but you're working to show how it can be your unique advantage?
3. Were you talked over or ignored by someone important, forcing you to develop more ability to empathise with others?

Order Copies of
The Silver Linings Storybook

Copies of The Silver Linings Storybook make a great gift, as well as a useful tool for fundraising organizations to give back while at the same time generating awareness and interest in your upcoming events & cause partnerships.

Coauthor appearances at your upcoming special events, and custom print runs including your own silver linings story or special message, are available for special events and bulk orders

TELL US MORE ABOUT THE PURPOSE OF YOUR UPCOMING EVENT:

_____

_____

PLEASE ALLOW MINIMUM 30 DAYS FOR FULFILLMENT OF CUSTOM PRINT RUNS

FULL NAME_____
ORGANIZATION
MAILING ADDRESS_____
CITY
PROV./STATE_____ COUNTRY_____ ZIP/POSTAL CODE_____

PRICING ($USD)	EACH	# OF COPIES	TOTAL	COAUTHOR NAME
1-4 COPIES	$34.00	_____	$_____	_____
5-49 COPIES	$30.00		$	
50-99 COPIES	$25.00		$	
100-499 COPIES	$20.00	_____	$_____	_____
500+ COPIES	$17.00	_____	$_____	_____

HTTP://THESPARKIFAGENCY.COM
DEBBIE.HOROVITCH@GMAIL.COM
416-533-2157

SECURE PAYMENTS BY PayPal
VISA MasterCard DISCOVER AMERICAN EXPRESS
No PayPal Account Required

Dream,
Share &
Enjoy.

www.ingramcontent.com/pod-product-compliance
Lightning Source LLC
Chambersburg PA
CBHW052215240426
43670CB00037B/631